MW01616869

THE

WAR
ON CHILDREN

How Pop Culture and Public Schools
Put Our Kids at Risk

KAREN L. GUSHTA, Ph.D.

CORAL
RIDGE
MINISTRIES

Fort Lauderdale, Florida

THE WAR ON CHILDREN:
How Pop Culture and Public Schools Put Our Kids at Risk
By Karen L. Gushta, Ph.D.

© 2009 Coral Ridge Ministries Media, Inc.

All rights reserved. Written permission must be secured from the publisher to use or reproduce any part of this book, except for brief quotations in critical reviews or articles.

All Scripture quotations are taken from the New King James Version. Copyright © 1982 by Thomas Nelson, Inc. Used by permission. All rights reserved.

Scripture quotation marked (NIV) is taken from the HOLY BIBLE, NEW INTERNATIONAL VERSION®, NIV®. Copyright© 1973, 1978, 1984 by International Bible Society. Used by permission of Zondervan. All rights reserved.

ISBN: 978-1-929626-59-5

Cover and Interior Design: Roark Creative, www.roarkcreative.com

Published by Coral Ridge Ministries.

Printed in the United States of America.

Coral Ridge Ministries
P.O. Box 1920
Fort Lauderdale, FL 33302
1-800-988-7884
letters@coralridge.org
www.coralridge.org

For the generations to come.

May we faithfully tell them

"the praises of the Lord,

And His strength and His wonderful

works that He has done."

Psalm 78:4

CONTENTS

ACKNOWLEDGEMENTS

Sitting in a Coral Ridge Ministries planning meeting and hearing Matt Krepcho, Director of Marketing, say, "I think Karen should write a book on education," I was stunned. Like many of the opportunities God puts before us, this was something I had wanted to do for years. But now it was on God's timetable—not mine. That meant, of course, that it was also a short one!

Therefore, there can be no doubt that this book could only have come about through the efforts of everyone on our Coral Ridge Ministries production team. My sincere thanks go to each one of them. They are ever a delight to work with, and their continual encouragement is sincerely appreciated.

Besides thanking Matt for giving me the opportunity and the push to write this, my thanks go to John Aman, Director of Communications and my department director, for allowing me the opportunity to work on this project uninterrupted and at home. My thanks go also to John, along with Bob Knight, for taking my plodding prose and making it more readable. Where it still suffers from the heaviness of a former academician's hand, I bear the blame. My heartfelt thanks to my department members, Andrew Scott and Nancy Britt, for joining John in praying daily for me as I was writing! Thank you also to Nancy and to Jennifer Busto, our lovely summer intern, for their diligent copy editing. Thank you to Barbara Meyer for her final check on copy and proofs—her eagle eye cannot be matched. Another sincere thank you is due to Barbara for negotiating deadlines with our design team and printer. In that vein, my thanks go to Roark Creative for the excellent work on the cover and interior design. They have captured the concept of the book well. And a warm thank you to Dickinson Press for working with us on changing timelines.

A special thank you goes to our Executive Vice President, Hector Padron, for his generous words of encouragement through this entire project.

My love and appreciation go to my husband, Richard, who is always encouraging. He entered into this project with unbounded enthusiasm and support. I am ever thankful that God brought us together to serve Him and to enjoy the blessings of marriage!

Finally, *"Thanks be to God, who gives us the victory through our Lord Jesus Christ. Therefore, my beloved brethren, be steadfast, immovable, always abounding in the work of the Lord, knowing that your labor is not in vain in the Lord"*(I Corinthians 15:57-58).

FOREWORD

In *The Abolition of Man*, first published in the 1940s, C.S. Lewis takes modern educators to task for alienating youths from their own heritage. This leaves the children vulnerable to harmful ideologies.

If you disarm a child with sustained doses of skepticism toward all things—including parents—you can plant ideas that will blossom later into full-fledged rebellion. Then the child/adult can be manipulated into man-centered "progressive" ways of thinking and acting.

Modern public education fosters coolness toward traditional loyalties, Lewis says.

> [Such teachers] see the world around them swayed by emotional propaganda—they have learned from tradition that youth is sentimental—and they conclude that the very best thing they can do is to fortify the minds of young people against emotion. My own experience as a teacher tells an opposite tale. For every one pupil who needs to be guarded from a weak excess of sensibility there are those who need to be awakened from the slumber of cold vulgarity.[1]

How much more so is this evident after years of miseducation and coarse, soul-deadening "entertainment" in the decades following the publication of Lewis's work? Who has not seen that hipper-than-thou, vacant look on groups of youths roaming the nation's malls in search of thrills, or anything to fill the void in their hearts? Some wear T-shirts with profanities or the single word "Whatever!" The latter is a white flag to the gods of cynicism, and an unwitting cry for help, although they would never admit to anything so uncool.

But little do they know, many of these kids harbor ideas that will harden into certainties that will shape their later worldview, and not for the better. And it's no accident.

"It is not a theory they put into his mind," Lewis writes of a typically hapless public school pupil, "but an assumption, which ten years hence, its origin forgotten and its presence unconscious, will condition him to take one side in a controversy which he has never recognized as a controversy at all."[2]

In her far-reaching and well documented book, *The War on Children*, Dr. Karen Gushta sounds the alarm that Christian children are not immune from this insidious trend. Their hearts and minds are up for grabs, and if they are not instructed in biblical truth and showered with love from parents and their church family, she warns, their hearts will grow cold until ignited by a substitute. This, she notes, is what Dr. D. James Kennedy described as "the religion of humanity."[3] Instead of a passion for Christ, and a love of America's rich heritage, children will be steered into a global worldview in which the government knows best and the birth of each child is seen as a net loss for the environment.

Think of teens you've seen in supermarket aisles, admonishing parents for not buying explicitly "green" products, such as the "right" light bulbs. Or sternly lecturing them on "tolerance" while showing no such patience with their parents' belief that marriage should be the union of one man and one woman, or that large families are a blessing.

Since faith and knowledge are the keys to obtaining wisdom, and the Book of Proverbs tells us to prize wisdom beyond earthly gain, it helps to know what forces are at work in order to respond properly and effectively.

In chapter after chapter, Dr. Gushta traces the history of public education, the daunting cultural challenges currently facing parents, and the fast-evolving new threat of one-world schemes designed to take power out of parents' hands and give it to global bureaucrats. From the secularist theories of the Unitarian, Horace Mann, in the 19th Century to the coldly effective *Rules for Radicals* by Saul Alinsky, and little-known ambitions of the federal No Child Left Behind program, to the growing authority of the United Nations' Convention on the Rights of the Child, Dr. Gushta's book is not for the faint-hearted. But then, neither is parenting, as Dr. James Dobson pointed out in one of his best-selling books. Nor is Christianity itself.

However, far from a hand-wringing tome that leaves the reader depressed, *The War on Children* returns again and again to the antidote: a renewed covenantal responsibility on the part of the larger church community to protect its children. Parents cannot do the job alone, Dr. Gushta writes, and to expect them to do so is not fair or biblical.

The most important education is that which shapes character. The Bible instructs parents to "train up a child in the way he should go, and when he is old, he will not depart from it" (Proverbs 22:6). This message is not only for parents. In Chapter 10, Dr. Gushta lays out the simple, yet profoundly important task of the church community:

> [Children] need the pure and powerful armature of
> the truth to protect them spiritually, mentally, and

emotionally from such assaults. Doing anything
less is not feeding His lambs—it is sending them
to the slaughter.

Dissecting curricula and educational trends, Dr. Gushta
shows why Christian parents cannot rely on church youth groups
and weekly worship to counter the daily flood of statist, secular
teaching and materials commonly found in government-
controlled schools. The overall thrust of public education, she
argues, is not merely neutral, but effectively anti-Christian. She
cites sobering statistics from the Barna polling group that show
many Christian youth lose their faith in later years, a stark
testimony to the impact of the one-two punch of government
schools and a hostile popular culture.

Education happens every day, all around us, Karen notes, so
we cannot cede ground to the enemy:

> We cannot forsake any cultural arena. Wherever
> the battle rages between the kingdom of Christ
> and the kingdom of Satan—that is where we
> must be raising the standard for Christ. Indeed,
> the battle rages through every social institution
> and in every part of culture and society because it
> rages in the human heart.

She aptly quotes Christian philosopher and theologian
Cornelius Van Til, who once wrote,

> He [the believer] knows that his cultural activity
> will not be in vain in the Lord. . . . He knows that
> he must fight the battle for a Christian culture
> first of all within himself and then with those

who seek to destroy his faith.

After making her case that the hour is late, the stakes are enormous, and that children represent not only our responsibility but our hope for the future of the church and the nation, she issues a challenge in the final chapter:

> Will we, too, go forth, as did the disciples, in the power of the Holy Spirit to "conquer the world of culture for Christ?" Will we join together as a band of brothers and sisters in Christ, willing to give our utmost for His Highest?

Anyone reading *The War on Children* will be convicted to do more to pluck kids out of the hands of those who would harm them—and will be empowered to do so as well.

ROBERT H. KNIGHT
Senior Writer and Washington, D.C.
Correspondent for Coral Ridge Ministries

Chapter One

WHAT WAR?

American culture is on the attack against our children. This war on our nation's children has resulted in the deaths of tens of millions of babies killed by their own mothers while in the womb. But the attack has not just been physical. The mental and spiritual lives of children and youth in our country have been under assault for decades. The barriers that should protect them from devastation and death have been broken down by the very cultural institutions that should be guarding them from harm. The adults of our nation are like the ostrich God speaks of in Job 39:13-16:

> The wings of the ostrich wave proudly,
> But are her wings and pinions like the
> kindly stork's?
> For she leaves her eggs on the ground,
> And warms them in the dust;
> She forgets that a foot may crush them,
> Or that a wild beast may break them.
> She treats her young harshly, as though they
> were not hers.

Indeed, it seems that we are now a generation that acts as if the young are not ours. Our culture is obsessed with "youth," yet parents do not know how to nurture their own children. They no longer give them the moral and spiritual guidance God expects them to.

There are endless facts supporting the claim that our children are under attack—this book will share many of them. But first let's think of who these young people are. They may be your own children, or your grandchildren, or your nephews and nieces, or even the children of friends and neighbors. I think of 19-year-old Gracie, of 15-year-old Eliot, of 12-year-old Haley, of 7-year-old

Genna, of 3-year-old Schuyler—the children of friends and relatives, of pastors and single moms. They are all the inspiration for this book. They are from a generation missing close to 50 million of their peers.

These are the children and youth who are now living under the full brunt of the war on children. They are living in a vulgar, coarse, and completely sexualized culture, where porn is so plentiful that 90 percent of them have viewed it online—most while doing their homework.[1]

They have even been called the "porn generation" by one of their own. At age 21, Ben Shapiro described what's happening to his generation in his book, *Porn Generation: How Social Liberalism Is Corrupting Our Future.* Ben started writing opinion columns at age 17, and when he was 20, he published his first book, *Brainwashed: How Universities Indoctrinate America's Youth.* Truly a *wunderkind*, Ben entered UCLA at age 16 and went on to Harvard Law School upon graduation. "Young Ben," as I would refer to him when reading another of his columns to my husband, writes with perceptiveness and wit. His commentaries on what's happening to his generation reflect the devastation of the minds and morals that is taking place among them.

In July 2008, at age 24, Young Ben got married. For years Ben had been referred to on the Internet not with affection, as "Young Ben," but with derision, as "Virgin Ben." Ben had, as an Orthodox Jew, remained abstinent throughout college and law school and had frequently advocated for it. Consequently, he was mocked and derided. In his column, "I Got Married Last Week," Ben wrote poignantly of his hope for the future—a hope that his children would grow up in a nation where families would be secure. For Young Ben, the question of who would lead America after November 2008 was "no longer a political question," it was a personal question. "Who will protect my family? Who will protect the future of my children?" he said, pondering the impending election.[2]

Who Is Protecting Our Children's Future?

As a childless Boomer myself, I do not think of the future in terms of what it will bring for my children or grandchildren, as do most of my friends. Attending the 30th reunion of my high-school graduating class, I had no stories to tell of what my children are doing, nor of the exploits of my grandchildren. My hope for the future is a vicarious one—something that I experience by noting the growth of my friends' children, or watching the young people from the 4th and 5th grade Sunday school class I taught move on into the church's youth group and choir.

When parents bring their babies forward for baptism in our church, the event does not spark a memory of my own children receiving the blessing of God's covenant. However, we are a part of this solemn ceremony nonetheless. When our pastor asks us as members of the congregation, "Do you promise before God to do everything you can to support these families, to model Christ, and to live the gospel in a way that honors God?" We respond with heartfelt affirmation. But I know that I will never fully appreciate what that family will experience as this young child grows to adulthood. I will not spend any sleepless nights caring for a sick one, or waiting up for one who has missed his curfew. I have no worries about what my child may be doing while on a sleepover at a friend's house. I have never faced the issue of whether to home school, or try to find the way to pay for my child to attend a Christian school; nor have I had to consider how I should deal with the perils of placing my child in a public school.

My point of view, therefore, in this book is not that of the concerned parent or grandparent who is aghast at what is happening to our children in the current culture. Nor am I speaking primarily as an educator—even though I was involved in education for most of my professional life. The perspective I've taken is that of a member of the Church—Christ's body, which itself is under attack by the secular media, a sex-crazed culture, and in government-run schools which have tossed out prayer and Bible reading and taken out all references to the Christian founding of our nation.

Attacks on our children have been assaults on us adults as well. But the role of the elder generations to protect and to provide for the younger ones has too often been compromised and ignored.

Although many try to rationalize away the effects of divorce on children, we know that it has a devastating impact. Only 68 percent of children under 18 now live with two parents,[3] and even at that, one parent could be a step-parent. Recent statistics show 60 percent of children under age 18 have experienced the breakup of their parents—some by divorce and some by the separation of cohabiting parents.[4] With family splits—comes greater risk for children living in poverty. In 2006, 42 percent of children living in families with a female head and no husband present were living in poverty, compared to eight percent of children living in married couple families.[5]

Adults have been pursuing their own pleasures of consumption and self-fullfillment. During the past decade, while we've been worrying about the threat of terrorists crossing our borders, our children have been under attack by another threat—a predatory culture that is insidiously and persistently destroying their lives.

The Faces of the Predators

What are the faces of those who prey upon our children? One is the leering face of the sexual predator despoiling our young through pornography—20 percent of Internet porn involves children.[6] An even more sinister form is the sexual assailant. Children are the most vulnerable victims of rape—60 percent of female and 69 percent of male victims report that they were first raped before age 18.[7]

In *Porn Generation,* Ben Shapiro unmasks the faces of the media, the entertainment world, and popular culture. He shows that behind the seductive smile luring teens into thinking that sexual activity is not only exciting—but something they should engage in—is a truly tragic face.[8] Magazines, movies, and popular music all create a fantasy world for teenagers—a world in which "hooking up" is the new norm. The dreadful result is that by the time they graduate from high school, 48 percent of our nation's teens have had intercourse, and 15 percent of high school students have had four or more sex partners in their lives.[9]

Prior to 1960, there were only two common sexually transmitted diseases. Now there are more than 30, and teenagers and young adults are the ones most vulnerable to infection. Approximately 12 million Americans get infected with STDs every year—nearly three percent of the entire population. Of that group, 63 percent are younger than 25 years old.[10] A study in 2008 found that one in four girls in high school is infected with a sexually transmitted disease—a finding that should truly alarm us all.[11] Those who have contracted a sexually transmitted disease—such as syphilis, chlamydia, or human papilloma virus (HPV)—may suffer the irreversible effects of these diseases: sterility, damage to the brain, heart, or blood vessels, or incurable genital warts.

Upon entering college, what may have been "exciting" can become threatening. Between 20 to 25 percent of women in college experience an attempted or completed rape.[12] We can assume that these figures would be vastly lower for Christian colleges. Yet, having firsthand knowledge of a young woman who was a victim of date rape while attending a Christian university, it is clear that these young women are also vulnerable.

The war on children is not only killing our children in the womb and infecting them with deadly STDs, it is murdering them outright. It should shock and stupefy us that homicide is the second leading cause of death for young people 10 to 24 years of age.[13] Furthermore, the heartbreaking fact is that of all juveniles murdered in 2007, 35 percent were under the age of five, with the most common method of murder being physical assault. At least 50 percent of the time, the murderers' weapons are their own hands and/or feet.[14] In some cases, those attacking children are their own parents or members of their families. Twelve out of every 1,000 children under age 17 suffer physical, sexual, emotional abuse, or neglect from, in the majority of cases, family members or family friends.[15]

While the above list shows all the kinds of physical attacks that put our children in danger, they are in jeopardy in another way as well. Parents who are making every effort to protect their children from physical violence in their neighborhoods and schools, often find it much more difficult to protect their children from the violence against their minds. Especially for Christian parents, the challenge to nurture their children "in the training and admonition of the Lord" may seem like an almost hopeless cause in the context of today's polluted culture.

The Loss of Our Christian Heritage and Values

Our nation seems bent on jettisoning the public and governmental symbols of our Christian heritage and denying its role in our history. Even the new Capitol Visitor Center in Washington, D.C., initially misidentified our national motto as "*E Pluribus Unum*" rather than "In God We Trust." Our President is steering our nation away from its Christian mooring. He has declared, "We do not consider ourselves a Christian nation or a Jewish nation or a Muslim nation. We consider ourselves a nation of citizens who are bound by ideals and a set of values."[16]

For some time now the Christian roots of those "ideals and values" that the President spoke of have either been ignored or distorted by the textbooks and curriculum in our government-controlled public schools. In some schools, not only are children told not to pray silently or to read their Bibles, they are forbidden to hold meetings for Christian clubs on campus, contrary to the freedom provided under The Equal Access Act passed in 1984 during the Reagan administration.[17] These school policies and curriculums are only symptoms of the real disease, however. The root problem is the view that schooling should be dominated by a secular outlook on life. As Dr. Richard Lappert and Dr. Robert Simonds point out, this form of education, "while pretending to be neutral, actually opposes the reality of God and His truth, and thus is doomed to fail even at its well-intentioned purposes."[18]

So, in addition to the malevolent and leering faces of sexual predators and pornographers, and the enticing face of sexual promiscuity, the other face we should fear is that of the benign, well-intentioned government policy maker or public school educators who fail to see that life is not "neutral." They work alongside the well-meaning, but misguided politicians and government bureaucrats who fail to acknowledge that all problems, whether they be social, political, or cultural, come under the sovereign rule and claims of Jesus Christ as Lord of all the universe.

The faces of those who fail to recognize Christ's claims as Lord of all may be benign, but their voices self-confidently proclaim that America's culture *is* and *should be* secular. They state with all sincerity that our nation would be better off if the Christian worldview, Christian morality, and Christian religion were silenced, suppressed, or merely sidelined from the public square and cultural venues. But, as Dr. Albert Mohler, Jr., points out in *Culture Shift*, "There is no genuinely secular state, no secular argument, and no secular motivation, even among those who consider themselves secular. There is no neutrality."[19]

This is the true foe that is destroying our children. Until we return to the founding vision of a republic governed by a moral and religious people—until we experience the renewal of our culture through the efforts of citizens whose hearts have been transformed by the gospel of Jesus Christ, the assault on our children—who are the future of our nation and the future of the church—will continue. As our culture becomes more vulgar, profane, and ungodly, children are its most vulnerable victims. They are always the first to suffer the attack, whether inside or outside the womb.

The Face of Revival—The Face of Youth?

Nevertheless, it is these children who may bring the revival that is our country's greatest need. There is evidence that the stirrings of the First Great Awakening, which preceded the American Revolution, "started among the young people in Jonathan Edwards' church at Northampton, Massachusetts, and then spread up and down the Connecticut River Valley in New England."[20] This was preceded by an earlier "Uprising of the Children" that started in the European region of Silesia along the Czech-Polish border. The historical account is written in "a 41 page tract published in London in 1708 with the long title (typical of the period), *Praise out of the Mouth of Babes, or, a Particular Account of Some Extraordinary Pious Motions and Devout Exercises, Observ'd of Late in Many Children in Silesia.*"[21] These "Pious Motions" started, according to Dr. Bruce Hindmarsh, professor of spiritual theology at Regent College in Vancouver,

> . . . when school-age children of Protestant parents were not willing, like their elders, to be silenced and marginalized by their Catholic rulers. The children at Sprottau . . . began to meet in the open fields outside the town at daybreak and two or three more times a day. They would form a circle and pray—sometimes lying prostrate—and then sing

Lutheran hymns, read Psalms and devotional texts, and close with a blessing. One Protestant father was so worried about the children doing this in defiance of the authorities that he tried to lock his son and daughter in their bedrooms. When he heard that they were going to climb out the window, he relented and let them go.[22]

From this children's movement, Hindmarsh connects the dots all the way across the Atlantic to Jonathan Edwards' Massachusetts.[23] But what strikes me is the description of these children—"sometimes lying prostrate." I think of the account (of which I have since lost track) describing the thousands of young people who prostrated themselves on another field last November. They came to Qualcomm Stadium in San Diego on November 1, 2008, to be part of a 12-hour prayer vigil on behalf of the passage of Proposition 8, the California Amendment to uphold marriage between a man and a woman.[24] Their prayers were answered, the amendment passed and has since been upheld by the California Supreme Court—to the surprise of many.

Is it time to take heed of the example of our youth? Is it time to join with them and to prostrate ourselves before the Lord to plead for Him to bring revival to our nation—not for our sake, but for theirs?

Chapter Two

TOO MUCH SCHOOLING, TOO LITTLE EDUCATION

For decades, Dr. D. James Kennedy followed the decline of schooling in America and the effect an increasingly secular system was having on children. In the late 1980s, as his television ministry grew, he warned the Church that educators were teaching a humanist worldview. His booklet, *Restoring the Truth*, documented how the "forum of the public schools" was being used to advance secularism and a "religion of humanity."[1]

Since then, the evidence has continued to mount. In addition to failing to teach a Christian worldview, America's schools are failing to teach our children the basic knowledge and skills they need. When compared to the children of other nations, America's children do not shine. As Ann Coulter points out in *Godless: The Church of Liberalism*,

> American students excel on international tests in fourth grade, the earliest grade for which international comparisons are available. But as American children spend more time in school, their scores decline. By the eighth grade, Americans are merely average in international tests. By the twelfth grade—having received all the benefits of an American education—they are near the bottom.[2]

There can be no doubt that our public educational system is moving everyone toward the lowest common denominator. This is just one reason our culture is "dumbing down" the level of discourse in the media and the public square. We're growing accustomed to absorbing information in sound bites. Rhetoric is winning the day over truth. Judge Robert Bork has pointed out that the educational system, driven by an ideology of egalitarianism, follows the "one size fits all rule." The prevailing notion, he says, is "that the education must be pretty much the same for all levels of ability."[3] The result—those with higher levels of academic talent are no longer pressed to achieve "excellence in all things," much less "all to the glory of God," as D. James Kennedy would say.

Few of us today could imagine coming out of our public school system at age 18 being equipped to pursue the curriculum that novelist Willa Cather studied at the University of Nebraska in 1891. As Judge Bork notes, she studied Greek (three years), Latin (two years), and German (one year) as well as Anglo-Saxon. She had to read Shakespeare and the Elizabethans; the 19th century writers Browning, Emerson, Hawthorne, Ruskin, and Tennyson; and French literary classics. Her university curriculum was rounded out with studies in history, philosophy, rhetoric, journalism, chemistry, and mathematics. Such a classically based education left her well-prepared to write such classics herself as *Death Comes to the Archbishop*, and *My Ántonia*.

Nowadays, there is an abundance of schooling, but the kind of education Cather received is hard to come by. Today's aspiring writers, such as one young friend of mine who is studying at an Ivy League school, find it hard to find meaty courses among the electives they are offered. Comparative literature choices include "Love Stories," "Male Friendship from Aristotle to Almodovar," "Beyond Fidelity and Betrayal: The Mysteries of Adaptation," or "Narratives of Theft and Theft of Narratives." The latter course includes Dan Brown's "classic," *The DaVinci Code*, among its major texts.[4]

Dangerous Professors Aren't the Only Problem

As Ben Shapiro shows in *Brainwashed: How Universities Indoctrinate America's Youth*, higher education has become indoctrination and "moral relativism is a widespread disease" on campuses. Leftist ideologues hold sway in classrooms, where they pursue partisan politics at every opportunity.[5] David Horowitz writes about some of the current crop of indoctrinators in *The Professors: The 101 Most Dangerous Academics in America.* Not surprisingly, he includes Bill Ayers, whose name was in the news during the 2008 election campaign, due to his association with then-candidate Barack Obama. Ayers, a radical, left-wing activist who is a Distinguished Professor of Early Childhood Education and Senior University Scholar at the University of Illinois, Chicago, has had considerable influence in the field of teacher education. In many ways, as we'll see in a subsequent chapter, he epitomizes what is wrong with teacher education in our country today.

In *Conspiracy of Ignorance: The Failure of American Public Schools*, Martin L. Gross lays responsibility for the decline of teaching and learning in America squarely at the feet of the educational establishment. Education bureaucrats, administrators, and academics wield control over: 1) teacher certification, 2) teacher training, 3) teacher unions, 4) teacher tenure, 5) terminal degrees for administrators—which include the Ed.D. degree that requires little academic knowledge, 6) school curricula, 7) and grading standards. State legislators, who hold constitutional powers over educational institutions in their states, are generally less than well-informed on these subjects. Furthermore, Gross claims that parents, PTAs, and school board officials have "abdicated their powers" to this establishment.[6]

Grade inflation, Gross says, is occurring at every level. I encountered it when I recommended that an elementary student be retained, as well as when I taught courses in higher education. Believing that one of my 5th grade students would have serious difficulties with 6th grade material, I recommended that she be held back. Her parents were not as distraught over it as was the girl. In the end, she was allowed to move on to 6th grade, primarily because she was physically more mature than most of her classmates, and it was thought that she would be subject to ridicule if she stayed in 5th grade.

By their college years, students no longer need parents to intervene and plead for changes in their grades. They have learned well the art of doing so on their own. During my final semester of teaching as an adjunct instructor, in each course I taught, at least one student tried to lobby me to change a grade—either on a paper or the course. When I spoke to administrators, their sympathies were clearly with the students.

Gross wrote his book in 1999, but the trend he documented was already clear to President Reagan's Blue Ribbon panel in 1983, when they wrote *A Nation at Risk*. In their oft-quoted assessment of our nation's schools, they stated, "If an unfriendly foreign power had attempted to impose on America the mediocre educational performance that exists today, we might well have viewed it as an act of war."[7] When Thomas Sowell wrote 10 years later about the educational establishment, he found that little had changed:

> The responses of the educational establishment to the academic deficiencies of their students today include (1) secrecy, (2) camouflage, (3) denial, (4) shifting the blame elsewhere, and (5) demanding more money.[8]

"My Kid's School Is Fine"

During my 17 years in teaching and teacher education in both public and private schools, I found that teachers often shifted the blame to parents. Teachers tend to agree with Gross that parents are "abdicating their powers" and abandoning the schools to bureaucrats and administrators. In every teacher education course we were required to provide information to our students about how to "involve parents." Although a number of factors prohibit parents from becoming more involved, including everything from apathy to overwork, another factor might be at play. As polls commissioned by the professional educators group, Phi Delta Kappa, have shown for years, the majority of parents truly believe there is nothing wrong with *their* child's school, unlike other schools across the nation.

This was confirmed again by the 2007 PDK poll. When parents were asked to "grade" their own child's elementary school, 61 percent gave it an A or B. But when it came to grading the nation's schools, only 16 percent gave them an A/B grade."[9]

Why the disparity? Authors David Kupelian and Gary DeMar point out that parents of children in government-run public schools seem to suffer from the "my kid's school is fine" syndrome, thus justifying their lack of concern about what is happening to their child during school hours. As Kupelian writes in *The Marketing of Evil: How Radicals, Elitists, and Pseudo-Experts Sell Us Corruption Disguised as Freedom,* there is an "aura of unbelievability" amongst all the bad news confronting parents that shows the hazards their children face in attending government controlled public schools.[10] DeMar, writing in *Whoever Controls the Schools Rules the World,* says, "My guess is that most parents have no idea what's going on in their child's school. If they don't hear any bad news, they assume that all is well." DeMar elaborates:

> Keep in mind that public school children are not comparing their education with the public school education that was prominent forty years ago. And it wasn't that great back then. The education students are receiving right now is normal for them. It's the only standard they know, and it's not a very good one. Anyway, a school that does not teach from a Christian perspective is at best

third-rate and dangerous.[11]

The Culture Is Hardwiring Our Kids' Brains

We will take a closer look at the educational establishment in subsequent chapters. We'll also consider the covenant role and responsibility of parents and the larger Christian community. But there is another aspect to the issue before us. While schooling from kindergarten through college is being "dumbed down," the culture has ramped up its "educational" effect on our children by means of media, entertainment, and popular idols and icons that influence children's worldview, belief systems, values, and ultimately their behavior.

We will look at the *educational effects* of our culture in greater detail in the following three chapters. Before closing this chapter, however, let's consider *why* we need to do so. In simplest terms, it has to do with the way children learn. Over the past 15 years or so, psychologists have discovered that we store information in our minds not only in the form of verbal concepts and words, but also in visual images and by way of what's called "kinesthetic" learning. This means that we often remember best those things that we participate in through some form of physical activity. It also explains why we can so easily recall stories and images we see in movies and on television and on the computer. These visual images are stored in our visual memory banks.

The implications of this are tremendous. As our children and young people spend greater and greater amounts of time watching TV, films, and sitting at their computers, they are developing brains that more readily respond to visual images than verbal concepts communicated through the written word. A University of New Hampshire professor noted that his students "tend to have an image-based standard of truth. If I ask, 'What evidence supports your view or contradicts it?' they look at me as if I came from another planet. It's very foreign to them to think in terms of truth, logic, consistency and evidence."[12]

Today's children and youth are not anchored in logic and reason as were previous generations. Therefore, youths can unwittingly hold self-contradictory notions, such as the view that there is "absolutely no absolute truth." However, although they do not respond to logic, they do respond to stories, myths, and legends. Consequently biblical epics and romances can capture their imaginations. The good news is that according to the 2009 survey of reading by the National Endowment for the Arts, reading rates are up for the first time in 25 years. Also, young adults (18 to 24-year-olds) showed the greatest increase in literary reading. Since 2002, reading among this demographic has increased by nine percent among both men and women. Novels and short stories are the current preferred genres.[13] This information should both encourage and challenge Christian novelists and short story writers!

Further good news—weekly Bible reading is also now at its highest level since plummeting to a 20-year low of just 31 percent in 1995. By 2000, this figure was up to 40 percent. The most recent data gathered by George Barna in 2006 showed that 47 percent of adults read their Bibles every week during a time other than church.[14] Barna did not study "occasional" Bible reading. According to a Gallup poll done in 2000, 59 percent of Americans said they read the Bible at least occasionally compared to 73 percent who said they did so in the 1980s. Hopefully, this percentage has also increased.[15]

As I will attempt to show in subsequent chapters, we need to do more than just change the way we *school* our children. Better curriculum and teaching methods, even putting our children exclusively in private Christian schools or homeschooling them, is not sufficient. We must educate them in a Christian worldview and establish them as committed disciples of the Lord Jesus Christ who have a comprehensive understanding of biblical truth. We must equip them to respond to and even engage with the darkening culture around us.

Cultural Education

For the very reason we discussed above, we must begin to think beyond education as something that takes place only in school settings. In its broadest sense, *education* is everything we experience and interact with in the environment around us. I am not advocating a Deweyan view that "experience *is* education." Neither am I talking about a behaviorist faith in the environment as the source of all learning. I simply want to emphasize that we must never forget that children are always learning through every activity in which they engage, whether it is directed activity or not.

Teachers, generally speaking, intend to teach by directing students' attention and activities. Parents direct their children's activities, but not always with the conscious intention of teaching them. Nevertheless, children are always learning. In its broadest sense, therefore, education takes place in any context where someone's attention and activities are directed. Sometimes that comes from sources in the environment, such as a TV, CDs, films, Xbox, or Wii. Whatever the source, as long as the attention is being directed and input received, learning is taking place. Thus, the culture educates over time as multiple inputs and messages are absorbed.

Nevertheless, the primary source for educational input for the majority of us is our *family*. As Henry R. Van Til observed in *The Calvinist Concept of Culture*, "The family is the smallest unit of society and the real fountain of culture. . . ."[16] Within the family we first learn by observing our mother and father and siblings and by interacting with our primary environment—our home. There is no doubt that a significant amount of learning comes from interacting with our physical environment. However, it is primarily by observing and imitating our parents' actions and words that we learn key moral and spiritual lessons that form the foundation of spiritual and moral beliefs. As George Barna points out, these beliefs are pretty well established by the time we are 13 years old[17]—the age when, in biblical times, a child entered adulthood.

This could be reason for discouragement among parents who take seriously the enormity of this task. However, as in everything, God always gives His people guidance through His Word. Thus, He has provided explicit instruction on how parents should educate their children. It is recorded in numerous places in the Bible; the first and clearest is in the book of Deuteronomy.

God's Instruction on How to Educate

Deuteronomy records three speeches given by Moses to the children of Israel before his death and their entry into the Promised Land. In the middle speech, recorded in chapters 4–26, Moses made an impassioned appeal to the people to be faithful to God's covenant with them, while rehearsing for them both general and specific stipulations of that covenant. Following a short introduction in chapter 4, Moses repeated the Ten Commandments God had given at Mount Sinai. He reminded them that they had asked of him, "You go near and *hear* all that the LORD our God may *say*, and *tell us all* that the LORD our God *says to you*, and *we will hear* and *do it*" [emphasis added] (Deuteronomy 5: 27).

Then, in Chapter 6, Moses gave them what is referred to as the "Greatest Commandment." [18] First he sets up the context:

> Now this is the commandment, and these are the statutes and judgments which the LORD your God has commanded to teach you, that you may observe them in the land which you are crossing

over to possess, that you may fear the LORD your God, to keep all His statutes and His commandments which I command you, you and your son and your grandson, all the days of your life, and that your days may be prolonged. Therefore hear, O Israel, and be careful to observe it, that it may be well with you, and that you may multiply greatly as the LORD God of your fathers has promised you— "a land flowing with milk and honey" (Deuteronomy 6:1-3).

Biblically speaking, Moses' exhortation to the people to *fear* the Lord (vs. 2) was an entreaty to give "reverence, awe, and respect"[19] to God by keeping His commandments. Notice too, that Moses was clearly speaking in intergenerational terms. Faithfulness to God is the expected response for *every* generation of those who are called and brought into a covenantal relationship with Him.

Then Moses delivered what Jesus later called the "first and great commandment" (See Matthew 22:37-38 and Mark 12:29-30).

Hear, O Israel: The LORD our God, the LORD is one! You shall love the LORD your God with all your heart, with all your soul, and with all your strength (Deuteronomy 6:4-5).

After setting out the standard of total love and obedience to God alone, Moses gave the people clear and explicit instructions as to *how* they should teach their children this command.

And these words which I command you today shall be in your heart. You shall teach them diligently to your children, and shall talk of them when you sit in your house, when you walk by the way, when you

lie down, and when you rise up. You shall bind
them as a sign on your hand, and they shall be as
frontlets between your eyes. You shall write them
on the doorposts of your house and on your gates
(Deuteronomy 6:6-9).

In the New Testament, Paul, the great apostle and teacher of
the basic doctrines of the Christian faith, wrote some simple advice
to the Philippian church—advice that is also fitting for parents to
give to their children.

The things which you learned and received and
heard and saw in me, these do, and the God of
peace will be with you (Philippians 4:9).

The Philippians had seen Paul in prison giving testimony of
Jesus and praise to God. They knew of his love for them and his
willingness to give of himself in every way for them. In all of their
relationships with Paul, the Philippians had been actively learning
from him and receiving his teaching. Therefore, he could exhort
them to take what he did and said—and do likewise. This form of
imitative learning is a fundamental way we all learn. It is the way
our children learn from us from the day they are born.[20]

In his letter to Timothy, Paul admonishes his son in the
faith regarding the role that Scripture should have in teaching
righteousness. According to Paul, it should be preeminent and
it should be the foundation for all true teaching. Paul reminded
Timothy that Scripture alone can direct his steps and correct any
deviation in his life from that standard of truth. In II Timothy 3:
16-17 Paul wrote:

All Scripture is given by inspiration of God, and is

> profitable for doctrine, for reproof, for correction, for instruction in righteousness, that the man of God may be complete, thoroughly equipped for every good work.

These Scriptures are among those that parents and teachers and all who work with children and youth should meditate on and ponder deeply. Their implications for our view of *covenantal cultural education* are profound. In chapter six, we will consider this in more depth. Before doing so, however, we must consider: a) how the culture is training our children's patterns of thinking and behavior by means of hidden worldviews in the media they consume; b) the general assault on the moral sensibilities of our children and youth by a sexualized consumer driven culture; and c) how all moral barriers are being pushed to the limit by the idols and icons of popular culture. These are the topics of the next three chapters.

Chapter Three

WORLDVIEWS IN DISGUISE

His penetrating wit has brought Rush Limbaugh such a following that Democrats have tried to label him as "the head of the Republican Party." Ann Coulter's acid pen, Jon Stewart's satire, Stephen Colbert's mockery, Bill Maher's cynicism, and Glenn Beck's self-mocking quips and skits all signify that political commentators are finding the comic terrain a friendly one.

For those who grew up in the 1960s and '70s, as I did, with the NBC evening news, the familiar, "Good night, Chet," "Good night, David," was nothing more than the close of a newscast. I never thought that the newscast I had just heard was a worldview biased toward a secular view of world events. Now, however, we all flag our own biases by our choice of news outlets. Which one is truly "fair and balanced?" With the addition of a myriad of sites on the Internet providing daily commentary on the news, we can find information on any topic written from any perspective we choose.

Having a buffet of news sources available does not mean that we are any closer to getting the truth. The worldviews propounded through these media outlets are most often secular and humanist, and in most cases, as Marvin Olasky documented in his 1988 book, *Prodigal Press,* they have a strong anti-Christian bias. Thankfully, Olasky and others decided to do something about this. The growth of *World Magazine,* especially in its Internet subscriptions, shows that Christians are looking for news and commentary that provide a Christian worldview perspective.

Nevertheless, the average reader of *World* is 51, and so Christian commentary is, for the most part, lost to our youth. Where do they go for news and commentary? Not to CNN or FOX, whose demographic base is closer to 60 than 50. As one self-described "new progressive" blogger noted, "Given what we know about the relationship of blog authorship to blog readership (same attracts same), it's possible that a major reason for young people turning away from TV news is that there aren't very many young people represented on news channels, except as criminals or objects of sin in one way or another."[1] We may dispute his reasoning, but there is no doubt that the blogosphere and You Tube are drawing the young. In 2006, 60 percent of You Tube's users were between 18 and 34 (close to 40 percent were 18 to 24).[2]

Reaching the 18 to 34-Year-Old

It's the demographic that Stephen Colbert claims to reach with his satiric reports of current news broadcast on cable television's Comedy Central Channel. What attracts young audiences to the political commentary of Colbert, Jon Stewart, and Bill Maher?[3] Besides the humor, which always attracts the young, it's a quality that Quentin Schultze identifies as *persona*. Schultze, a Christian professor of communications, has written several books about "medialand" intended to help parents "win their kids back from the media."[4] Facial image and dialog establish each TV personality's *persona*—the element that gives us a feeling of personal connection with the people on the small screen. The fact that viewers are often dismayed to see their "friends" go off the air when a TV series ends is "only manifestation," Schultze notes, "of the human craving to follow individuals, to trust them, to admire them and sometimes even to commit one's life to them. Television satiates that craving for some people because of its emphasis on *persona*."[5]

Both Stephen Colbert and Jon Stewart have strong TV personas that, along with their satire, sarcasm, and mockery, make them particularly appealing to their target audience of 18 to 34-year-olds. However, don't think that their goal is simply to "entertain." As Stephen Colbert claimed at the end of an interview with Muslim convert Cat Stevens (aka Yusuf), "I'm here to educate."[6] Jon Stewart likewise "educates" his audience by bringing on guests to talk about topics such as health care reform or CIA briefings. Both men adeptly poke fun at much of what deserves to be satirized, but their continual use of sexual innuendo and double entendre pegs them on the darker "infernal" side of the humor spectrum, as Louise Cowen points out in her masterful introduction to *The Terrain of Comedy.*[7]

Like Colbert and Stewart, Bill Maher's humor abounds with sexual innuendo. In comparison to Stewart's sarcasm and Colbert's mockery, Maher is coldly cynical. As his unsuccessful foray into filmmaking, *Religulous,* showed, behind his satire is a moral relativism that compels him to try to make all religions morally equivalent and, wherever he can, Christians look silly and ridiculous.[8]

Ridicule is a favored tool of the political far Left. Its use was popularized by Saul Alinsky in his political action handbook, *Rules for Radicals.* Liberal politicians who grew up in the '60s studied Alinsky, as did Hillary Clinton, who wrote her Wellesley graduation thesis on Alinsky in 1969.[9] Likewise, Barack Obama used Alinsky's methods during his early career as a Chicago South Side community organizer, for Alinsky was a master of using grassroots activism to promote political ends.[10] Alinsky's Rule #5 is: "Ridicule is man's most potent weapon. There is no defense. It is irrational. It is infuriating. It works as a key pressure point to force the enemy into concessions."[11] When Christian bashing isn't successful in suppressing or silencing the Christian viewpoint, *ridicule* is used to sideline it.

"Silent" Shaping of Youth Opinion

The degree to which the media are acting as the "silent shapers" of the opinions of our youth can be seen in David Kinnaman's and Gabe Lyons' book, *UnChristian: What a New Generation Really Thinks About Christianity . . . and Why It Matters.* To research the beliefs of the millennial generation—those between 16 and 29 years of age—the authors interviewed 440 young people. Among those interviewed, 59 percent said that their view of Christianity was formed by their experiences at churches, 50 percent by their acquaintance with Christians, and only 31 percent said visual media contributed to their view of Christianity. Significantly, however, the predominant views held by these young "outsiders" to the Christian faith were that Christians are hypocritical, too focused on getting converts, anti-homosexual, sheltered, too political, and judgmental.[12] The authors conclude that indeed, "young people are unaware of the 'silent' shaping of media in their lives. People often underestimate the role of media in their thinking and behavior."[13] There can be no doubt that youths today are ingesting "worldviews in disguise" and their ability to recognize and discern, much less evaluate, these competing worldviews is limited.

What we also must recognize is that the worldviews they are picking up from media are competing with what they are learning from parents, pastors, and teachers. As Quentin Schultze points out,

> Each of these groups of traditional authority figures is increasingly distraught over the apparent power of the media to shape youth's values and beliefs. Unless parents are wise about the opportunities as well as the liabilities of media use, parenting will be transferred to communications moguls, media conglomerates and media idols. It's time to win back our children without trashing the wonderful gifts the new media can bring.[14]

While youth respond to satire and mockery, it's lost on children, who respond more readily to silliness and clowning. The media, however, have continued to push the boundaries in children's entertainment. Today it often wears a patina of childish play and silliness, but underneath, its humor is strictly adult, as signaled by the trademark double entendre. Even Disney cartoons feature curvaceous female heroines that are far from childlike.

However, it's not just sexualized content for which parents must be alert. They must also be on the lookout for the worldviews that are subtly slipped into the story. Evolution is one of the most pervasive worldviews found in children's entertainment, as Carl Kerby shows in his book, *Remote Control: The Power of Hollywood on Today's Culture*. Jimmy Neutron, SpongeBob SquarePants, and a host of children's television, movies, and books are all riddled with this religious worldview.[15] In addition, homosexual characters and themes are now commonplace.

Nevertheless, all media can be used to start a conversation that can lead to identifying the worldviews contained in it. It can be done, as we read in Deuteronomy 6, when "you sit in your house" and watch a DVD together, or "when you walk by the way," after going to the theater. It can't be done, however, if your child is watching the DVD alone, or if you do not find the time to talk with your son and daughter about the movie they saw with friends at the theater. Reading together what Christian critics say about the movie may also give your teens something to share about it with their friends.

As Carolyn Moynihan noted on her blog, *Family Edge*, "Parent power can really work, starting at the home front, where gentle persuasion backed by a bit of research could convince teens they deserve better than puerile crassness for their hard-earned cash."[16]

Using the Power We Have to Shape the Culture

Just as it is a myth that government-run schooling is "neutral" and does not oppose the reality of God and His truth, the claim that entertainment is "value neutral" is also a myth. Entertainment's "educative effects" on our children cannot be underestimated.

Industry heads, like the late Jack Valenti, former president of the Motion Picture Association of America, wanted films to be evaluated on technical excellence and creativity, not content or moral values.[17] But, as Robert Knight points out in *Age of Consent: The Rise of Relativism and the Corruption of Popular Culture,* "spiritual neutrality is a fatal conceit" and it will only bring down God's wrath on those who are "wise in their own eyes" (Isaiah 5:21).[18]

What kind of "education" do our children receive from entertainment and media? As Knight thoroughly documents, they learn that there is no absolute truth and no ultimate moral values; therefore, we are all free to pursue whatever sensual pleasures appeal to us. "Relativistic thinking has penetrated many Western institutions and shattered norms, nowhere more than in popular culture. Sex and violence, and the pursuit of material success have become dominant elements in films and television shows," Knight writes.[19] Television producers' abandonment of the "family hour" 8 p.m. time slot to programs that include crude language or sexual situations shows the "cavalier attitude that some Hollywood people take toward children—and teenagers—many of whom are watching at that hour and cannot be monitored every moment."[20]

The 1990s were not a good time for family friendly TV, as the Media Research Center documented in a 1995 study.[21] With President Clinton's escapades in the White House being splashed across the news in 1998, teens soon learned that oral sex was not truly "having sex." Teens who participated in oral sex, but didn't have intercourse, considered themselves still to be "virgins," and a survey of college students by the American Medical Association showed that 60 percent claimed that oral sex was not "real sex."[22] Sadly, the genital herpes and other STDs they were picking up from it *were* real.

Along with more profanity, vulgarity, and sexual themes during times when children and families are viewing television is, for the most part, sidelining Christianity. Programs make "religion seem unimportant," as Knight says.[23] Unless, of course, that religion is New Age. While commercials regularly show people "meditating" or doing yoga, TV personalities such as Oprah Winfrey promote their favorite New Age guru, like Eckhart Tolle. But even Oprah's endorsement shouldn't fool anyone that New Age is just a new disguise for a form of the occult that denies God as the Creator separate from His creation. It teaches, instead, that all humans are part of God and just have to look inward to unleash their divine powers.[24]

There is hope, however. When parents and the public put enough pressure on the Federal Communications Commission (FCC) to impose stricter standards to protect children and provide family friendly viewing, the FCC does respond. Public outcry has worked in the past. The FCC leveled a $550,000 fine against CBS for airing the Janet Jackson Super Bowl "reveal." The fact that she had a strategically located "decoration" on her breast, should have made it clear that it was not a "wardrobe malfunction," as CBS claimed. The case has now gone to the Supreme Court, since the Third Circuit Court of Appeals threw out the FCC's fine in July 2008.[25]

It is quite possible that the High Court will reverse the Third Circuit's decision in the case against CBS. In April 2009, the Court upheld an FCC decision that Fox Television violated decency rules in 2002 and 2003 when participants used obscene expletives during awards ceremonies. Judge Scalia noted that the broadcasters can now easily use technology to bleep out offending words.[26] This should be an encouragement to contact the FCC the next time you're watching a program that pushes over the line by using profane or obscene language.

Now is the time to keep up the pressure on the Federal Communications Commission to impose stricter standards. It's easy to lodge a complaint by phone, e-mail, or letter. Before contacting them, try sending an e-mail directly to the offending TV program. I was happily surprised to find that when I complained about the high number of double-entendre "zingers" on one of the early morning shows, they stopped! Supporting watchdog groups[27] who are fighting for higher standards on our behalf is also vital. (This endnote gives FCC contact information.[28])

In addition to recognizing both the opportunities and the liabilities of media use, we also need to understand the power we have when we vote with our wallets by refusing to patronize media we find unacceptable. Instead, we can support the efforts of Christian filmmakers who are endeavoring to make movies that uplift and show the power of Christ's redemption. In order to do this, we need to become informed by reading Christian movie guides and finding out whether a movie is suitable for children, regardless of whether it is being marketed to them. And here's the good news—such pressure actually works!

A Message of Hope and Redemption

Ted Baehr, who produces *Movie Guide*, which rates current movies on language, violence, sex, and nudity, noted in an interview,

> There are two sides to Hollywood. Sixty percent of the films are independent, but they produce only 10 percent of the box office. Usually—but not always—they are the ones producing the "ugly" movies. The major studios produce 40 percent of the movies, but they get 90 percent of the box office. The majors have moved significantly away from foul language, etc., in recent years.[29]

Part of the reason may be that moviemakers have been getting the message from parents, media watchdogs, such as Ted Baehr,[30] and other groups that are voicing their displeasure with profanity in family-rated entertainment. Baehr reported in an article in *The Wall Street Journal*,

> Once again, family-friendly, uplifting and inspiring movies drew far more viewers in 2008 than films with themes of despair, or leftist political agendas. Sex, drugs and antireligious themes were not automatic sellers, either. Among the 25 top-grossing movies alone, 14 out of 25 had strong or very strong Christian, redemptive and moral content, and nearly all had at least some such content.[31]

According to Ted Baehr's research, Americans are supporting movies with messages of free enterprise, patriotism, and significantly, faith and values over those with left-wing, politically correct, atheist, or licentious and libertine themes—in some cases by as much as 30 to 1. The success of the movie *Fireproof*, which made over $6.5 million on only 839 screens its opening weekend, shows how much our vote means at the box office as well as the ballot box. Although *Fireproof* was panned by some critics for being a "message movie" because of its Christian content, it is obvious that Americans have an appetite for messages of hope and redemption. Although Hollywood may snub such movies at the Oscars, as Baehr points out, it cannot do so at the box office. "Not if it wants to keep its fancy houses, cars, and planes."[32]

Reaching those with an appetite for hope and redemption through Christ should be a priority for every believer. We can use the very media used by the purveyors of perversion to connect with disconnected Millennials who are jaded by the senseless culture around them. Josh McDowell, well-known author and Christian apologist, has set out to reach youth by using Twitter and Facebook. Others are posting their testimonies of grace on YouTube. One of the most compelling is the story of the young couple who gave birth to a baby with the severe genetic disorder trisomy 18, rather than aborting their child.[33] Their video, which has had over two million views, is just six minutes long. But it is a powerful story of the preciousness of every life, and the redeeming power of God's love to turn heartbreak into that hope. Yet some want government regulation of the Internet that would require an ad for Planned Parenthood at the end of such a story.[34] It's imperative that the public spaces and platforms where this message can be shared and communicated stay open.

What Can One Person Do?

As Brian Fisher has pointed out in *Media Revolution: A Battle Plan to Defeat Mass Deception in America,* "Hyperbole, sarcasm, and deception are common tools of people who are puppets of the MMD [media of mass deception]. While such attacks lack serious thought and reason, the intent to drive all Christian expression from the public square is very real."[35] In his book, Fisher gives a number of suggestions for ways that Christians can get involved to keep the public square open.

At times it seems that all our efforts to change or influence the media are fruitless. We continue to see vulgar and obscene humor or programs that bash Christians, Christianity, or Christ. Nevertheless, we must remain proactive in this arena so that the Christian viewpoint is not silenced or sidelined in our society. We must be like the Old Testament figure Shamgar, whose accomplishments are recorded in one verse in the book of Judges.

Dr. D. James Kennedy tells the story of Shamgar in the chapter "The Sin of Aiming Low" in his book *Turn it to Gold.* Shamgar lived during the time of the judges, when Israel was living under the subjugation of the Philistines. Not only had the ungodly Philistines taken every one of the Israelites' weapons, they had deported all their blacksmiths so they couldn't make more. The Israelites were so despondent and lacking faith that they stopped planting their crops and were in hiding from the Philistine's marauding bands. Everyone, that is, except Shamgar. He plowed his field with his ox and planted his crops. Then, sure enough, the Philistines appeared just as his crop was ready for harvest. Rather than give up, however, Shamgar took his ox goad and killed the 600 Philistines who had come to ravage his home and steal his crop.

An ox goad is not a very impressive weapon. It was just the limb of an oak tree—about eight feet long, with a sharp iron point on one end and a flattened piece of metal on the other. As Dr. Kennedy tells the story,

> It certainly would have been easy enough for Shamgar to do nothing. Think of the many excuses that were readily at hand. *They are soldiers, and I am just a farmer. I don't even have a sword. There is really nothing I can do. I have to just let them come in and do as they wish.*
>
> But that is not what Shamgar said! Because of the faith he had in God ... because of the concern he had for his people ... because of his own dignity as a human being ... he decided to take a stand, come what may. As the Philistines swooped down, Shamgar took that ox goad and began to swing.
>
> There must have been some astonished Philistines that day! Eight feet of solid oak, with iron implements at each end, in the hands of a sturdy, enraged, faith-filled servant of God—the Philistines must have thought they had wandered

into a hive of angry bees. They were getting it from all sides, being jabbed and cut and pounded. And when the dust had settled, the six hundred Philistines lay dead on the ground, and Shamgar went back to his harvest. The Bible notes with eloquent simplicity: "and he also delivered Israel" (Judges 3:31).[36]

In the face of all the attacks of ungodliness against us, we may think, "What can one person do?" Instead, let us think of Shamgar, who took up the only weapon he had and was used mightily by the Lord to defeat the enemy.

Chapter Four

THEY BANNED PRAYER AND PROTECTED PORN

Porn has been big business in America for years. Americans spent $10 million on pornography in 1973. In 2000, they were spending $10 billion a year.[1] In 2006, according to Family Safe Media, the Internet pornography industry alone was generating $12 billion dollars in annual revenue, more than the combined annual revenues of ABC, NBC, and CBS.[2]

When it comes to Hollywood and pornography, author Ben Shapiro concluded in 2005 that,

> It's impossible to overestimate the amount of oversexed content coming out of Hollywood over the past decade. But it's not just the explosion in nudity among stars or the weakening of standards that have had an impact on the porn generation. There's a deeper message . . . as Hollywood has embraced the graphic elements of pornography, the moral relativism behind these themes has become an implicit message in nearly every major mass-market film. For films targeted at youth, these messages are often explicit.[3]

The impact of pornography on children is staggering. *The Washington Post* editorialized in 2004 that "more than 11 million teens regularly view porn online."[4] A study in 2005 by the Henry J. Kaiser Family Foundation found that only 23 percent of parents had rules about what their children were allowed to do on the computer, and only 25 percent of 7th to 12th graders said their home computer had a filter or parental controls.[5] Children and youths who use computers with no filter can easily access porn sites, only three percent of which require adult verification before entering.[6]

Protecting Kids From Porn on the Internet

So far, efforts to get laws in place to protect children and youth from online pornography and predators have not been successful. Congress has passed two bills—the Communications Decency Act (CDA) of 1996, and the Child Online Protection Act (COPA) of 1998. But when the laws were challenged by the ACLU and others as "government censorship," the federal courts have either struck down the law (as in the case of the CDA) or upheld an injunction by a lower court against implementation of the law—as was most recently the case with COPA. After the U.S. Court of Appeals for the Third District struck COPA down again in July of 2008, the Bush Administration asked the U.S. Supreme Court to review the decision of the lower court. In January 2009, the Supreme Court announced that it would not do so.[7]

There is little, if any, hope that the Obama administration will take any action to revive COPA or to push Congress for new legislation that would survive the courts. In fact, as Robert Knight has noted in his most recent book, *Fighting for America's Soul*, President Obama's Deputy Attorney General David Ogden "has a long record of serving the porn and abortion industries and the radical homosexual lobby. He even filed a brief defending a child pornographer in a 1993 case that got Attorney General Janet Reno reprimanded by both houses of Congress"[8] because her Justice Department failed to defend the conviction when it was challenged. Knight notes that Ogden has an extensive record of "issuing briefs on behalf of the ACLU, pornographers, abortionists, and homosexual pressure groups."[9]

As the second highest-ranking official in the Justice Department, the Deputy Attorney General "advises and assists the Attorney General in formulating and implementing Departmental policies and programs."[10] At the beginning of his career, Ogden served as a law clerk for Supreme Court Justice Harry A. Blackmun, best known for his ruling in *Roe v. Wade* that the so-called "right to privacy" gives women the right to kill their unborn children. Protecting "privacy rights" seems to be Ogden's *cause célèbre.*

Although there is little hope, as noted above, of getting any form of the Child Online Protection Act (COPA) passed again until Congress and this administration change, there is one related law that we should make sure is vigorously enforced. The Children's Online Privacy Protection Act of 1998 (COPPA as distinguished from COPA) became federal law in April 2000.[11] It applies to the online collection of personal information from children under 13 years of age. In this case, the concern for "privacy rights," which was used perversely by the Supreme Court in *Roe v. Wade,* has provided a measure of protection for children using the Internet. Among its requirements, COPPA identifies what websites must do to protect children's privacy and it places restrictions on website marketing to those under age 13.[12]

The COPPA protections against marketing to pre-teens are one way of dealing with increasing abuses in this area. Businesses have identified pre-teens as a potential marketing demographic worth tens of billions of dollars. In a recent commentary, "The Hostile Takeover of Childhood," John Whitehead notes that kids as young as 18 months recognize company logos and are asking for products by brand name by the time they are two years old. The pressure to turn children into materialistically minded consumers is affecting every potential marketing venue.[13]

Nevertheless, the fact that advertisers are targeting younger family members can be used in a positive way. Christian activists have been successful in getting programs off the air that violate family viewing standards. They have gone directly to advertisers and protested their sponsorship. Family brands are especially sensitive to the public's perception that they are being hypocritical by supporting such programs.

We should continue to push for significant government action against Internet pornography. Every household with children should have Internet filters. Accidentally accessing pornographic images devastates a young child's mind. Once viewed, these images cannot be erased. They can be replaced, but they will always be lodged in the mind's memory bank to be evoked or recalled in the future. Pornography is *toxic* and, like poison, all children should be protected from it.

Defenders of the Indefensible

In the book, *Indefensible: 10 Ways the ACLU Is Destroying America,* author Sam Kastensmidt shows how the American Civil Liberties Union has systematically been "defending the indefensible—protecting all forms of licentiousness and striving to destroy the boundaries of common decency."[14] Now the ACLU is attempting to remove porn filtering software that is required by federal law in schools that receive federal financial aid. The ACLU filed a case against public schools in Knoxville, Tennessee, for "blocking access" on school computers to homosexual and transgender websites that the ACLU calls "educational." There is no doubt such sites are "educational." The question is—in what way? The conservative American Civil Rights Union (ACRU), whose mission is to "protect the civil rights of all Americans by publicly advancing a constitutional understanding of civil rights," points out that in this case, the ACLU wants students to have access to thousands of websites. These sites include "sexually explicit text on almost every one, and sexually explicit photographs or graphics on many of them."[15]

Even if the courts rule that porn filters must remain on school computers, that does not mean our children will be safe from "sexually explicit content" in their schools. Sex education classes in government schools already "desensitize" children and youth to sex talk. "Much of the teaching done in sex ed classes is designed to break down the natural inhibitions of children toward sexual matters," say authors Frank York and Jan LaRue. "No sense of morality is attached to premarital sex, oral sex, homosexuality, and so on. In fact, to oppose any kind of sexual activity is to be considered intolerant."[16]

York and LaRue say the inclusion of such forms of "sex education" in government schools is due in part to the general decline in morality in our culture. They also point out that the philosophy behind the material used, as well as the materials themselves, comes directly from groups that advocate promiscuity—Planned Parenthood and the Sexuality Information and Education Council of the United States (SIECUS).

> Both of these groups have a radical agenda that is designed to stimulate an obsession with sexual activities. Planned Parenthood ... promotes what it calls "sexuality education," which is *nonjudgmental* and *explicit*. It has launched an attack against abstinence education, which it labels "fear-based education." SIECUS is firmly committed to promoting unrestrained sexual activities for children. In its publication, "Girls and Sex," this group says, "Sex play with boys ... can be exciting, pleasurable, and even worthwhile ... it will help later sexual adjustment."[17]

Putting Sex "Education" Into Practice

The newest fad among teenage girls is to send nude photos of themselves via cell phone. Called "sexting," this disturbing trend shows that they are clearly absorbing the lessons of their sex education classes. The ACLU has quickly stepped in to "protect the rights" of adolescents to engage in such behavior, but there is already a case of a girl committing suicide after her picture circulated all over her school and beyond. In another case, 20 girls caught sexting in one high school were given the option to attend classes on sexual harassment and sexual violence in order to avoid criminal prosecution. While 17 of them agreed to the penalty, the parents of three of the girls defended their actions saying "they were just having fun."[18]

Why are children and teenagers experimenting with sexuality at younger and younger ages? Zachary Gappa, Director of Research for the Center for a Just Society, concludes, "The answer is to be found in the culture in which they have been raised." Advertisers, news media, sociologists, and even teachers are all pushing sex in our culture. "Worst of all," says Gappa, "parents are complicit in all of this."

> They accept [the] idea that their children will act-out sexually and that there is nothing to be done about the barrage of sexual images fed to them every day. Yet these same parents relinquish their duty to discipline their children or teach them restraint. Even basic ideas of self-denial and maturity are now seen as harsh or abusive.[19]

It is clear that the moral compass of our nation has shifted dramatically. Neither government schools nor parents, in many cases, are protecting children from the tsunami of sex flooding our culture. Abstinence education, the surest way to teach teens how to protect themselves from the devastating consequences of sex outside of marriage, is set to be scrapped. The Obama administration's budget redirects funds from abstinence-only programs to "evidence-based and promising teen pregnancy prevention programs."[20]

What does the "evidence" show? It clearly demonstrates, according to Robert Rector of the Heritage Foundation, that abstinence programs that include a virginity pledge "dramatically lower rates of teen births," and abortion rates, teen sex, and out-of-wedlock births all decrease among teens who have made such a pledge. Although not all teens keep their pledge, this form of abstinence education results in the "number of sexual partners down a third to a half, compared to kids from a similar socio-economic background."[21]

Judicial Activists Ban Prayer

Judicial activism by the courts has also contributed to moving the nation away from God and toward greater immorality. In *The Supremacists,* Phyllis Schlafly shows how activists on the Supreme Court started in the 1960s to wage war on the public acknowledgement of God in our nation, first by banning school prayer in *Engel v. Vitale.*[22] As William Murray points out, "Prayer is a cultural marker. It is indicative of issues much larger than itself. The removal of prayer from public schools is one facet among many of the pervading secularism of our culture."[23]

We're not going to change the culture by reinstituting prayer in the government schools, but this decision marked a turning point in the Court's attitude toward religion. In his dissent, Justice Potter Stewart noted,

> The Court has misapplied a great constitutional principle. I cannot see how an "official religion" is established by letting those who want to say a prayer say it. On the contrary, I think that to deny the wish of these schoolchildren to join in reciting this prayer is to deny them the opportunity of sharing in the spiritual heritage of our nation.[24]

Not only has the Court continued to misapply the establishment clause of the First Amendment in subsequent decisions, any opportunity in government schools to share in "the spiritual heritage of our nation" has all but vanished since the high Court handed down this pivotal decision.

If the Supreme Court had stopped its attack on prayer with *Engel v. Vitale,* the effect might have been fairly minimal. However, as Schlafly documents, the judicial activism that began with the Warren Court (1953-1969) has become a hallmark of subsequent Supreme Court decisions involving prayer and the posting of the Ten Commandments in government schools. In 2003, the federal courts began to extend prayer bans to adults. The Fourth Circuit U.S. Court of Appeals and the Supreme Court let stand a lower ACLU-inspired court decision that made officials of the Virginia Military Institute personally financially liable if they reinstated the supper prayer: "Now O God, we receive this food and share this meal together with thanksgiving. Amen."[25]

Judicial Activists Promote Porn

Supreme Court judicial activists have directly contributed to the degrading and coarsening of culture by loosening the controls on pornography suppliers. This was done, as Schlafly shows, through a series of anonymous decisions handed down by the Warren Court. Schlafly doesn't mince words:

> Judicial supremacists are to blame for allowing a torrent of obscenity to engulf the movies, television, the theater, books, and even classroom curricula. Robert Bork observes that "the suffocating vulgarity of popular culture is in large measure the work of the Court. The Court did not create vulgarity, but it defeated attempts of communities to contain and minimize vulgarity."[26]

In 1966 the Court changed the obscenity test from requiring "social importance" to "social value." This was justified by the argument that the obscene *Fanny Hill* had "social value" because the prostitute, whose acts are described in detail through the entire book, reformed at the end. This let the pornographer's "nose in the tent."

The obscenity racket got into full swing after this decision, notes Schlafly, and by October 1966, dealers were flooding the Supreme Court with appeals from lower court convictions.[27] Backed by great financial resources and ensured of success by the presence on the bench of liberal activist justices Earl Warren, William Brennan, Abe Fortas, Hugo Black and William O. Douglas, they pushed forward. By 1970, the Warren Court had handed down an astonishing total of 34 decisions that "gave extraordinary victories to the pornographers, reversing all the judges, juries, appellate courts, and law enforcement officials connected with those cases." [28]

In unprecedented fashion, none of the justices of the Court wrote or signed individual opinions on any of these cases. All were *per curiam* (by the Court), making them a major legacy of the Warren Court. "Most of these decisions were only a sentence or two, an unusual tactic which enabled the Court to conceal from public debate the substance of what the Court was approving." Schlafly notes, "One has to search out the lower court decisions to see what gross obscenities the Court was wrapping in the First Amendment."[29]

The Role of Presidents: A Study in Contrasts

The Courts are not alone, of course, among government officials pushing our culture toward moral relativism by gutting the standards set by communities, states, and even Congress. Various presidential administrations have either chosen to enforce or not to enforce laws against pornography. For example, the

Lyndon Johnson and Richard Nixon administrations recommended loosening legal restrictions on pornography.

In contrast, President Reagan asked his attorney general, Edwin Meese III, to lead a distinguished commission to study the impact of pornography. The Meese Commission published a 1,960-page report in 1986 that documented the harmful effects of pornography and the connections between pornographers and organized crime. Porn industry supporters, including Barry Lynn, formerly of the ACLU and since 1992 executive director of Americans United for Separation of Church and State, attacked the report as biased and inaccurate.[30]

Since then, the pendulum has swung with each administration. President Clinton's Attorney General, Janet Reno, was famously "missing in action" on this issue, while John Ashcroft, George W. Bush's first Attorney General, met with anti-pornography activists early in the Bush administration, but did little to enforce the laws. Again, with David Ogden as the current deputy attorney general, there is little hope that the Obama administration will prosecute offenders.

Banning Porn and Promoting Prayer

Metaphorically speaking, our culture is living at the foot of Mount Sinai. We celebrate orgies and ignore God's commands. Our worship of the golden calf of materialism has led parents to forsake parenting and media moguls to use sex to sell worthless and vulgar movies, TV programs, and books. We have become desensitized to the coarsening effects of sin, and the exponential growth of sexual hedonism across our culture no longer shocks us.

As Archibald D. Hart observes in *Thrilled to Death: How the Endless Pursuit of Pleasure Is Leaving Us Numb*, one of the consequences of sexual hedonism is that people no longer have the capacity to experience true joy. Hart has actually coined a term for this—*anhedonia*—which he defines as "the reduced ability to experience pleasure."[31] The irony of our pleasure-seeking society is that it must ramp up the intensity of pleasures with each new experience in order to find some degree of satisfaction—witness the growth of *extreme sports* among the youth. This also accounts in part for increasing levels of violence and pornographic content in movies, etc.

For the Christian, our truest and greatest pleasure is found only in Christ, who alone can fill the God-sized hole in our hearts. As Augustine affirmed in the first paragraph of his *Confessions,* "You stir man to take pleasure in praising you, because you have made us for yourself, and our heart is restless until it rests in you."[32] The sensual, sexual, and sinful pleasures that contemporary culture has crafted to seduce our youth are leaving them jaded and lost, as Ben Shapiro has documented in *Porn Generation.*[33]

There is hope in Christ, however, for both pornographers and the porn generation. He forgave prostitutes—(*porne* in the Greek) and proclaimed that because they believed John the Baptist's call to repentance, they would enter the Kingdom of Heaven ahead of the chief priests and elders of Israel who had ignored the warnings of John (Matthew 21:28-32). However, the Bible is also very clear that those who do not repent of their *porneia*—sexual immorality— will not find an inheritance in Christ's Kingdom. As Ephesians 5:5 states, "For you may be sure of this, that everyone who is sexually immoral or impure, or who is covetous (that is, an idolater), has no inheritance in the kingdom of Christ and God."

Therefore, as parents, as grandparents, as godparents, and as fellow members of the church, it is our duty to use every means to warn our children and youth of the ungodliness of pornographic content. We must explain to them how watching, listening, reading about, and engaging in sexual activity before marriage corrodes their souls and jeopardizes their intimacy, bonding, and spiritual union with their future spouse. "Hooking up" with anyone other than one's own husband or wife leaves broken links of emotional pain and hurt which never fully heal.[34] Therefore, the vow of abstinence and chastity before marriage is truly God's primary plan for His sons and daughters.

May the day come again in America when we *ban pornography* and *promote prayer*—for the sake of our children and youth—and for the sake of our nation!

Chapter Five

HEROES AND HEROINES: VIRTUE AND VICE REDEFINED

We all love a good story, and when a powerful tale is told on film, it becomes twice as compelling. A well-told story—in print or on film—can lift us up and give hope of redemption, forgiveness, and joy. It can also take us down and show us the depths of sin and debauchery.

The most powerful stories, to be sure, are found in the Bible. Taken as a whole, the Bible is God's great epic, spanning all of human history and human experience. We find in it the romance of God's creation of Adam and Eve in the Garden, the supreme tragedy of mankind's fall through their sin, and the drama of Christ's conquest of sin through His redemption of sinners.

The cast of heroes in the Bible is as varied as are the villains that populate its pages. Many of the Bible's leading characters are ones with whom children can identify. Take the story of the young girl Miriam, who went to Pharaoh's daughter and arranged for her mother to be baby brother Moses' wet nurse. Or the story of 17 year-old Joseph, who was envied, falsely accused, but eventually exalted by the Pharaoh of his day. There are the stories of the courageous shepherd boy David, of young Daniel and his three friends, and of the young boy who braved the crowds around Jesus to tell Andrew of the five loaves and two fish he was willing to share. Children enjoy stories such as Paul's courageous nephew, who told him of the plot against him; Philip the evangelist's four daughters who prophesied; and even young Eutychus, who fell from a third story window as Paul preached late into the night!

But the stories of heroes that we can share with our children do not end with the Bible. Throughout history we find an abundance of heroes of faith: Augustine and Patrick, Jan Hus and John Wycliffe, Lady Jane Grey, John Bunyan, Amy Carmichael, and so many others whose stories should be familiar to our children.[1] Where are the stories of these brave figures in our culture today? They are either missing or rendered by Hollywood as anti-heroes, as in the 1985 Richard Gere version of *King David.*

The champions our children look up to today are mostly pop-culture sensations experiencing their 15 minutes of fame. These modern heroes are tarnished and heroines are ravished. As Adrian and Steve Rogers point out in *Family Survival in an X-Rated World,*

> In their quest for someone to admire, kids often mistake idols for heroes. Today's pop stars, movie idols, and superstar athletes fill the most admired list of teens, yet they openly warn, "Don't expect me to be a role model."... The entertainment world and cultural elite prescribe what is cool and what is not, yet refuse to be held accountable to any standard of behavior or morality. Instead of being heroes, when it comes to having a life truly worth emulating, they are indeed zeros.[2]

The Trend Toward Anti-Heroes

Who likes an anti-hero? Whether it's Tom Hanks in the movie, *Angels and Demons,* or Tony, the foul-mouthed gangster-in-therapy of *The Sopranos*—which collected 21 Emmy and five Golden Globe awards for "bringing a greater level of artistry to the television medium" during its eight season run—we no longer expect much from these "heroes" who parade through our TV programs and films.

Madeleine L'Engle, award-winning children's author and teacher of writing to hundreds of people, forthrightly voices her aversion to anti-heroes:

> Children don't like anti-heroes. Neither do I. I don't think many people do, despite the proliferation of novels in the past few decades with anti-heroes

for protagonists. I think we all want to be able to identify with the major character in a book—to live, suffer, dream, and grow through vicarious experience. . . . We don't want to feel *less* when we have finished a book; we want to feel that new possibilities of being have been opened to us.[3]

Heroes have come on bad times in our culture, as Peter Gibbon found out when he started researching his book, *A Call to Heroism: Renewing America's Vision of Greatness*, in 1992. When interviewed in 1999, Gibbon had come to the conclusion that,

In America, we no longer have public heroes. Politicians speak in platitudes and squabble. Corporate leaders downsize, then increase their own salaries. *Journalist* has become synonymous with *cynic*. Lawyers are seen as business-seekers, not as problem-solvers, and doctors as wary technicians. Soldiers press buttons, athletes are mercenary.[4]

According to Gibbon, "The word *hero* has been out of fashion since the late 1960s as a term to describe past or present public figures."[5] This should not surprise us. The media's rush to the bottom started in the '60s, although a relativistic outlook already controlled American culture before that, as Robert Knight documents in *The Age of Consent*.[6] And, as Diana West explains in *The Death of the Grown-Up*, the gyrating rhythms of 1950s rock 'n roll set the stage for the sex-drenched culture that followed. The teens who rebelled against adult sensibilities that inclined toward Frank Sinatra and Duke Ellington soon entered college and became the vanguard of the "anti-establishment" takeover of popular culture.[7]

Not Heroes—But Victims

The '60s marked two significant watersheds for media standards. First, as we saw in the previous chapter, 1966 was the year the Warren Court opened the floodgates to pornography in every medium with its *Fanny Hill* ruling. Second, when Jack Valenti became president of the Motion Picture Association of America (also in 1966), the first thing he did was junk the Hays Production Code, which had set the standard for voluntary self-regulation by the movie industry since the 1930s.[8] With the loss of the Hays Code, the *heroic* in Hollywood content was gone with the wind and, as Frank Capra wrote in his autobiography in 1971,

> The winds of change blew through the dream factories of make-believe, . . . The hedonists, the homosexuals, the hemophilic bleeding hearts, the God-haters, the quick-buck artists who substituted shock for talent, all cried: "Shake 'em! Rattle 'em! God is dead. Long live pleasure! Wife-swapping? Yea! Liberate the world from prudery. Emancipate our films from morality!"[9]

For a short time after September 11, 2001, *heroism* made a comeback in American culture. We spoke with awe and appreciation and used the word *hero* to describe firefighters and policemen, as well as the passengers who stormed the cockpit of United Flight 93. It seemed Americans were beginning to question their entrenched cynicism, apathy, and their preoccupation with celebrities and sex. We affirmed, for a time, Ralph Waldo Emerson's observation that "Times of terror are times of heroism."[10] But now, eight years later, as we scan the cultural horizon, it's hard to find any true heroes or heroines. They are *unfashionable* in a culture that has returned to admiring celebrities like Oprah Winfrey, who told graduating Duke University students, "[I]t is really fantastic to have your own jet."[11]

The *anti-hero* reigns once more. Media accounts of our conflicts in Iraq and Afghanistan have not profiled heroes, but largely victims. The mainstream media tells the stories of former football star Army Ranger Pat Tillman, who was the victim of friendly fire in Afghanistan, and Jessica Lynch, the 20-year-old Army supply clerk, who was heroically rescued from her captors in Iraq. But it was Jessica, not her rescuers, who became the focus of media interest. That interest intensified when pornographer Larry Flynt claimed that he had bought nude photos of her in order to keep them from being published.[12]

How can we expect anything else? For decades, authors such as Howard Zinn, whose textbook, *A People's History of the United States,* has sold a million copies, have told students "the Cold War was our fault as much as Russia's, American soldiers fought in Korea to prop up a corrupt dictator, and Vietnam was not a blunder but a crime."[13] Although books such as Coral Ridge Ministries' *Ten Truths About America's Christian Heritage*[14] clearly show the Christian roots and unique founding of our nation, a dark view of America's past dominates the media and government-run public school classrooms.

Even our current President has stated his "nuanced" view that America is no different from any other nation in believing its founding and heritage make it "exceptional."[15] Rather than viewing our Founding Fathers as heroes—men of courage and strength of character—children learn that Thomas Jefferson had children by a slave mistress, and George Washington's slave ownership negates his other incomparable accomplishments.

This trend toward anti-heroes and victims is discernible in

today's biographies. Gibbon notes that biographers now minimize people's achievements so they look like mere "ordinary people benefiting from a few good breaks." Our society honors the victims of history rather than its leaders. The word *hero* has been democratized and Americans admire "a range of people" who can be their *role models* or even *mentors*, but not their heroes. Next to the 19th century monuments of Abraham Lincoln and Puritan elder John Bridge that stand in Cambridge Common, the citizens of Cambridge, Massachusetts, recently added a sculpture honoring the victims of the Irish potato famine.[16]

But victims are hardly heroes. As Ralph Waldo Emerson said, "The hero cannot be common, nor the common the heroic." But when they are, says Gibbon, who has been an educator for most of his life,

> It can strip the word of all sense of the extraordinary.
> It can lead to an ignorance of history, a repudiation
> of genius, and an extreme egalitarianism disdainful
> of high culture and unappreciative of excellence.[17]

Without heroes, we have no models to emulate. "I try to convince audiences that we need models," Gibbons advises. "We're imitative creatures. We need to look up and admire!"[18]

Visions of Greatness—Visions of the Kingdom

In an earlier chapter, we noted Judge Robert Bork's claim that the trend toward "extreme egalitarianism," of which Gibbon speaks, is responsible in great part for the dumbing down of our schools and the lack of excellence in curriculums. One of Gibbon's favorite heroes, the British educator Sir Richard Livingstone, said, "True education is the habitual vision of greatness."[19] Not only do government schools fail to give children and youth any substantial "visions of greatness," but the popular culture is supplanting the visions we held in the past with nightmares of coarseness and vulgarity. *Celebrity* has replaced *heroism* as the basis for "greatness." Our cultural icons have more in common with the final days of Rome than the glories of Greece—much less the heroism of our Founding Fathers.

Civic education in America's schools should enlarge the vision of our youth by teaching them stories of heroism from our nation's founding. Sadly, however, there is an abysmal lack of such instruction, as the Intercollegiate Studies Institute has shown in three major studies since 2006.[20] When Peter Gibbon visited Yale University, he found plastered on the pedestal of the statue of Revolutionary War hero Nathan Hale an announcement of an undergrad "Ho and Pimp" party. Ironically, given the Supreme Court's role in changing the course of schooling in America, even some members of the High Court are concerned about the lack of good civic education for the nation's youth. Both retired Supreme Court Justices David Souter and Sandra Day O'Conner are advocating for improving American civics education.[21]

Nevertheless, knowledge of America's heroes and a strong civic education are not sufficient to strengthen and save the American republic. The gospel must be preached throughout the land. And if it is to prevail, as it did in the days before America's founding, when it lit the fires of liberty across the colonies, it will be up to the coming generation to carry this vision to our nation. But if the children of God's covenant-keeping families are to be captured by this vision for America, they must first gain a vision of their own place in God's kingdom. They must have a largeness of vision. This can only truly come when they see beyond personal horizons and glimpse the epic story of God's kingdom in action throughout history—from creation until Christ and from Christ to the present. Our covenant youth must have a personal sense of God's hand in history—always working, whether we see it or not—to bring about

His sovereign will and plan.

This broad kingdom vision can give coming generations a biblical perspective on present troubles and fortify them against fearful times in the future. The challenge we face as the church, however, is not just to engrain this kingdom vision into our children. We must also defy the incredible coarseness and vulgarity of the culture that surrounds them. If only we could protect them from its toxic effects by isolating them like the Bubble Boy! As we'll see in the next chapter, we need to provide a kind of *cultural education* that prepares them to "be strong in the Lord and in the strength of his might" and enables them "to stand against the schemes of the devil" (Ephesians 6:10, 11).

The Redefinition of Virtue and Vice

In *The Age of Consent*, Robert Knight observes that our culture has been steadily moving away from the value of *self-sacrifice*, which is an essential trait of the heroic character, to the egocentric "search for self-fulfillment." It started in the '40s and '50s, when commercialism began to have sway and divorce became more commonplace. "No longer were people viewing this world as a way station, but as a final destination," Knight says.[22]

And while the culture was moving toward the idolatry of *self*, the church was softening its message, no longer preaching the biblical understanding of man—that he is, by nature, sinful and in a state of rebellion against God and, therefore, needs a sinless Redeemer. America was drawn to a less offensive view—"the liberal view that man is good by nature and that the fulfillment of each person's desires outweighs any other claims on his time or loyalties."[23]

This liberal view has now found its full expression in our culture's admiration of those who have overcome "victimization" and achieved personal fulfillment—even wealth and fame—by their own efforts. Oprah Winfrey is the one of America's "most admired women." Likewise, Judge Sonia Sotomayor's biography was touted at her nomination to the Supreme Court because she had risen above the circumstances of a poor immigrant household to achieve success as a federal judge. It is not self-sacrifice that epitomizes these women's biographies, but self-fulfillment of their "dreams."

It was telling when Mother Teresa's and Princess Diana's funerals were held the same week in 1997. The former received minimal media coverage, while the latter was covered virtually non-stop for days. Princess Diana fits America's picture of a *heroine*; Mother Teresa does not.

The Boomer generation, which clearly reflects this striving for *self-fulfillment* and is so loathe to do anything requiring *self-sacrifice*, is now bequeathing its "me first" attitude to the next generation— constantly telling them they are "the best." It may be well-meaning, says author Colleen Carroll Campbell, but all this indoctrination in self-esteem by baby boomer parents, teachers, and media gurus has resulted in a generation brimming with pathological narcissism. So much so that many in the rising generation excuse rule breaking while claiming to be "satisfied" with their own ethics and character. The common view of today's youth is, "When it comes to doing what is right, I am better than most people I know."[24]

This high rate of self-satisfaction among teens who openly confess to lying and cheating may shock parents, but it doesn't surprise the authors of *The Narcissism Epidemic: Living in the Age of Entitlement*. Jean Twenge and W. Keith Campbell conclude from their research that Americans, especially the young, are suffering from "corrosive narcissism."[25] Colleen Carroll Campbell sees clear evidence of the consequences of this "fixation on indulging and exalting oneself."

> [Consider] the five-fold increase in plastic surgery and cosmetic procedures performed in the past decade, the greedy overconfidence that drove our

> mortgage meltdown, and the self-absorption that leads senators, celebrities, and ordinary citizens to habitually post their most trivial musings on Twitter and believe that the rest of us care which game show they watched on television or which burrito they ordered at Taco Bell.[26]

According to Colleen Carroll Campbell, researchers Twenge and Campbell have "taken some heat" for their analysis of narcissism in today's society, but "narcissist" might best describe the anti-heroes that predominate in our culture today. One can even make the case that this disease of the spirit penetrates all the way to the White House, where a young politician persuaded millions of Americans that he was ready to lead, despite a stunning lack of achievement, a tendency to exaggerate his accomplishments, to expect constant praise and admiration, to express disdain for those he considers inferior, and to set unrealistic goals. According to experts, these are all textbook symptoms of a narcissistic personality disorder,[27]

Where Are the Parent-Heroes?

Adrian and Steven Rogers do not hesitate to lay the challenge of providing good models at the feet of parents.

> It is the challenge of parents to help their kids sort out the difference between idols and heroes; to help them realize that those who are admired simply because of how they look, what they sound like, or how high they can jump, are often the ones who make the biggest mess out of their lives.
>
> It is also the challenge of parents to teach not only by word, but by example. You can't lead your

kids somewhere you have never been yourself. Determine to become someone they can look at and think, *I want to be just like you.*[28]

In their book, *Family Survival in an X-Rated World*, father Adrian and son Steve present "Seven Steps to Becoming a Hero to Your Kids." These include:

- A Godly Example
- Unconditional Love
- Constant Encouragement
- Wise Instruction
- Reasonable Restriction
- A Listening Ear
- A Happy Environment[29]

Aware as I am of how often I have failed to follow these seven steps during my teaching career, I can well imagine how parents might feel when reading this list. No doubt you can easily think of numerous times when you fell short and consequently were far from being a hero in your son's or daughter's eyes. But the beauty of this short, easy-to-read paperback is that the Rogers introduce these steps early, and then explain how to carry them out in the remaining chapters and appendices.

Giving our children godly heroes is an essential part of developing in their souls an enlarged vision of Christ's kingdom and their place in it. In his book *Christian Bashing*, Dr. Gary Cass provides a list of heroes who have defended the Christian faith throughout history. Starting with the apostles in the early church through the early church fathers, to the reformers and the apologists of the modern period, Cass shows that none of these men could sit idly by and allow the church of Jesus Christ to be attacked or the gospel defamed. He concludes,

> The Church has always defended itself against the attacks of an unbelieving world. Many of our greatest Christian heroes are the apologists and defenders of the faith, evidencing great moral and physical courage, while asserting the Christian faith's rich intellectual heritage. The Church cannot stand by as the truthfulness of the Christian faith and its values are attacked by its enemies and diminished by its critics. Defamation of our Lord, His Word, and His people must not go unanswered. The fashionable sport of Christian bashing demands a robust response.[30]

We not only need Christian heroes who are apologists; they must also be evangelists. In his passion to reach the lost with the good news of the gospel, Dr. D. James Kennedy used every type of media, including television, radio, print and even concerts performed in his church, both to expose the culture's lies and half-truths and to present the marvelous gospel of the Lord Jesus Christ. So too, we must faithfully continue to use every form of media to assert the rich heritage of Christianity's contribution to American culture, morality, and civic life, and to call to repentance those who sit in darkness. If the coming generations are to continue this work, we must show them the great Christian heroes and heroines who have brought the greatness of the power of Christ's redemption and the gospel's light and healing to every part of society, both here and across the globe.[31]

When our children and youth see their parents as heroes who are willing to give and sacrifice for their well-being; when they learn of the heroes and heroines in the Bible; when they become versed in the lives and teachings of heroes who have defended Christianity throughout history; when they count as friends those who have taken that faith to those who are sitting without hope in darkness, then our children and youth will begin to see themselves as heroes of the coming age—fully equipped as "His workmanship, created in Christ Jesus for good works, which God prepared beforehand that we should walk in them" (Ephesians 2:10).

This all begins when our children's hearts are anchored in God's love for them. The greatest romance, the greatest love story in the world, is the story of the Groom who came to rescue his Bride from certain annihilation and everlasting death. We were the lowest of the low, the meanest of the mean, the ugliest of the ugly; we were the true anti-heroes. Yet, Christ has lifted us up. He has reversed all our meanness and given us a new heart filled with His love. He has cleansed us, washed us, healed our ugly sores and wounds, and clothed us in beautiful wedding garments of righteousness, so that we could be His lovely Bride!

This truth is the wellspring of our desire to serve in love the One who sacrificed Himself in love for us. The anticipation that one day we will see our Heavenly Hero's face and finally be united with Him gives us courage and fortitude, no matter how little of the light of His face is reflected in the culture. It also gives us the courage to live lives of self-sacrifice, so that His redeeming power can be brought to every corner of the globe.

Chapter Six

COVENANTAL EDUCATION: MODELING KINGDOM DISCIPLESHIP

Christian parents face an almost impossible task in protecting their children from the influence of popular entertainment and media. Even the "news you can use" deals with STDs, drunk driving, rape—including gang rape and date rape, drugs, and more.[1] There's no plastic bubble we can encase our kids in until maturity that will protect their minds and hearts from the immorality and relativism that pervades our society.

On the other hand, Christian parents may not be all that concerned about the impact the media have on their children if their Christmas spending habits are an indicator. It's a little surprising that born-again Christians spent more than $1 billion on CDs, DVDs, video games, and magazines for their children under the age of 18 during the 2007 Christmas season. And this was in spite of the fact that many parents had misgivings about the moral content of these items.[2]

We've already shown how American culture *educates* our children. Movies, TV, and other media are indeed forming and shaping their worldviews and character. Pollster George Barna found that the Millenials—young adults under 25—are "more than twice as likely as all other adults to engage in behaviors considered morally inappropriate by traditional standards." When he compared these young adults to Boomers (not a group known for its high moral standards), Barna found the following comparisons:

- Use of profanity in public—Millennials 64%, Boomers 19%
- Engaging in sex outside marriage—Millennials 38%, Boomers 4%
- Lying—Millennials 37%, Boomers 6%
- Getting drunk—Millennials 25%, Boomers 9%
- Viewing pornography—Millennials 33%,

Boomers 16%.[3]

So, many Boomers may not necessarily be providing a poor example to their children, but are they expecting their kids to follow their good example? Diana West, who has studied Boomers for 10 years, has concluded that they are not:

> The very odd fact is, Boomer (and Boomer-plus) parents today expect, prepare, and even enable their youngsters to encounter and engage in a welter of antibourgeois, even criminal, activities. These range from a berserk kind of sexual adventurism, to the mortal dangers of mind-altering drugs and alcohol. They include a spectrum of rude, crude, and formerly socially unacceptable behaviors, such as what is still known as, even in these value-neutral times, "bad" language.... Certainly, it's not every kid who engages in such practices, any more than it is every parent who enables him to. But it's something to reckon with that every kid is unavoidably and indelibly marked by them.[4]

What are we to do in the face of the relentlessly rising tide of immoral behavior and moral apathy, not only here in America but in Europe? The moral toxicity of our culture makes the prospect for our children's future look bleak. We are bequeathing them a nation drowning in debt so large we can no longer grasp it conceptually. In 1989, when D. James Kennedy preached the sermon, "Christianity and the Federal Deficit," our national debt was $3 trillion. Now it is almost four times that amount![5] In his 1989 sermon, Kennedy said, "What we are doing to our grandchildren is so criminal that I wouldn't be at all surprised if the younger generation today says, when it reaches maturity, 'Phooey on the whole bunch of you! And just cuts us all off.'"[6] What would he say today?

Not only are we forging chains of debt for our children and grandchildren, we're also putting them in slavery of another kind. On our watch, our constitutional republic is being replaced by an army of unelected bureaucrats who make decisions that impact us all and which we have no recourse to recall by the power of the vote. Furthermore, our nation's leaders are either paralyzed by fear of offending our enemies, or they are strangely deluded into thinking that apologies for past "offenses" will defang and pacify rogue regimes. But anyone who still doubts that militant Islam is inflamed with global ambitions (an obligation laid on all Muslims in the *Koran*) should quickly seek to better inform himself on this topic.[7] If ever there were a time when our nation needs real heroes, men and women of character, conviction, and courage, it is in America today!

Changes Across the Generations

As we saw in the previous chapter, Americans by and large no longer admire or aspire to be heroes. Our contemporary heroes are not those who have shown *self-sacrifice,* but rather those who have achieved *self-fulfillment.* It was not so with Americans who grew up before the age of television. "The previous generations found their heroes not only from the media, but also from direct experiences, friends/siblings, and parents' occupation."[8]

These included members of the "Greatest Generation," so named because of the bravery and everyday heroism they displayed in defending freedom against the threats of Nazism and Communism, whose leaders sought world dominance. Today we are deluding ourselves into thinking that the threats we are facing are not similar in nature.

As I was writing this chapter, celebrations were being held

for the 65th anniversary of the Normandy Invasion. I watched the ceremonies at Omaha Beach and listened to the stories of men who left their landing crafts on that day with every expectation that they might never get off the beach. Yet thousands jumped into the water, many never making it to shore.

We "Boomers" rightly call the generation that fought in World War II "the Greatest." We have earned our generational moniker not because of anything we have done, but simply because we came along with millions of other babies born after these soldiers came home to their wives. As a Boomer, I listen with amazement to the stories of my father's generation—of those who fought in the various theaters of the war. Dad's younger brother John was one of those who went up Omaha Beach on the second wave. I recall his telling us the story while we sat around his kitchen table only a short time before he would move into a care center with his wife. Remarkably, none of the men in his unit were killed either that day or in the following days, as they fought their way toward the Rhine—a fact Uncle John attributed to God's divine protection. Initially, some of the men scoffed when he stood up to pray for them. Gradually, even the scoffers became silent as they pressed toward their goal without experiencing casualties.

Like Uncle John, who directed fire at enemy fortifications in Normandy, my father directed artillery fire for the landing of American forces on the island of Okinawa—the bloodiest campaign of the war in the Pacific. Dad, like so many others, rarely spoke of his wartime experiences. I did find out, however, that he too, was ridiculed for his faith—and so it was a special time when he was able to connect, while on the island of Luzon, with some of his band of Christian brothers from Calvin College who had been drafted or enlisted. But, as with so many who returned home changed by the war, my dad was never able to return to his goal of becoming a pastor like his older brother Henry, whom he so admired.

Despite the valor and sacrifice of their fathers, the Boomer

generation that followed rebelled against the values the Greatest
Generation lived and died by. Diana West explains what happened
when the Greatest Generation came home from the war.

> There is a certain poignancy, and even mystery,
> to the fact that these victors in an epic world war
> returned home to lose a domestic culture war that
> would climax in the 1960s. That is, these many
> millions of men may have returned from Europe
> and the Pacific to head traditional households and
> drive postwar prosperity, but they were also put
> to pasture culturally in no time. . . . Generational
> power shifted, marking maybe not the end of
> a way of life, but certainly the end of a way of
> living—the end of growing up.[9]

West goes on to show that our society's fascination with the
youth culture started during the 1950s. By the mid-'50s, rock 'n
roll was taking over popular music. In addition, teenagers had
new consumer power because of America's prosperity. Rather
than contributing, as earlier generations had to their family's
needs, these teens took the money they earned after school or
during summer jobs and spent it on themselves. They went to the
movies and bought records and teen magazines—a totally new
phenomenon. They also showed the same fascination with media
and communication devices that today's teens have—buying
telephones and record players which, of course, they kept in their
own rooms.

What was the result? For the first time in history, a "teen
culture" developed. Thus, although the 1950s are often
characterized as a very "family-oriented" time, something was
happening that would have profound consequences. The family

quickly became a kind of "second-class citizen" among the social institutions in American culture. Schools, media, and even the marketplace were grabbing space and power to influence the lives of youths. The consequence, as Steven Mintz points out in his book, *Huck's Raft: A History of American Childhood,* was that these institutions "fostered separate worlds of childhood and youth... from which parents, and even older siblings, were excluded."[10]

Ironically, according to West, the first generation to develop a separate youth culture has also been famously loathe to leave it and move on to maturity. Boomers, in their striving to live in a kind of "perpetual adolescence," have refused to grow up and assume the role of upholding traditional norms of morality and virtue. Instead, they, more than any other generation, have been responsible for what West calls the "death of the grown-up" and the endless pursuit of youthfulness.

Boomer parents, according to West, have essentially abdicated their role, and they now have a different view from past generations about "what it means to be in charge of a child's welfare."

> Children attend R-rated movies—with their parents in charge (or with a parentally approved "R-card" that allows children in sans adult). Children sit on sex education advisory committees—also with their parents in charge. One such committee in Montgomery County, Maryland, included among its advisers an eleven-year-old girl, someone still eligible to order from a kiddie menu. . . . Society takes it on itself to rule out garlic and cayenne as being too spicy for her years (think: kids' menus), but not birth control methodology and polymorphous sexual experimentation.[11]

Without "grown-ups," where can our children find the role models and mentors, much less the heroes, who will help guide them through that painful process of "growing up?" More importantly, where will the church find those who will help them to grow into spiritually mature disciples—followers of the Lord Jesus Christ?

Teachable Moments

There's a popular concept among teachers—the *teachable moment*. It's an unplanned opportunity to teach a concept or principle in an especially powerful or poignant way. Such moments can't be planned; they are serendipitous. They provide the setting for a lesson that is spontaneous, unexpected and unscripted.

When I read Deuteronomy 6:6-8, I see God exhorting parents and all who teach children to consider *every* moment that we are with children as *teachable moments*. In other words, we are to be on the lookout for opportunities to give personal testimony and examples of God's marvelous mercy and grace, or to point out His spectacular power and majesty, or to identify His unfailing love and sovereign rule of all creation. We are also to make sure such moments occur in the course of our daily activities with our children.

Speaking through Moses, God makes it very clear that parents are to use every chance they have—when they sit, walk, lie down, and rise up again—to talk with their children about God's greatest commandment, the command to love Him with *all* our heart and *all* our soul and *all* our might.

As we develop family traditions and plan family times together, whether they be "treats" or "tasks," we can use such times to present stories that illustrate a truth about God's nature, His creation, or His ways, so that we touch our children's hearts with truth in a unique and tender way. *Teachable moments* give the chance to engrain a truth seen in a symbol, a metaphor, or an illustration. They provide visual images and the kinesthetic memory of an event that will be evoked many years hence by a word, a song, a scent, or a passing reference to that event, and call forth remembrance of the principle, the truth, or even the lesson taught.

Each time such a moment is used to teach, to train, to model, it anchors the child's heart and understanding more securely. The picture of God's goodness and kindness, which stretches so far beyond our understanding it cannot be fully penned, becomes more and more complete. It begins first with the simplest of outlines and shapes and gradually fills in with rich hues and subtle details that capture the imagination and enlarge the comprehension of who God is, what He has done for us, and what He has called us to do.

My husband observed one such family tradition while on one of his several treks overseas. For a time he stayed in the home of a Christian lay pastor who was ministering among the Tamil tea plantation workers in the hills of Sri Lanka. In this exotic setting, he made a remarkable discovery about Christian family life which should be commonplace. Having no Christian family background, Richard was amazed at the strength of their family bonds.

It was their custom that whenever father, mother, son, or daughter got ready to leave the house to go out on business or an errand, everyone would gather around that person for a moment. Whatever they were doing, all would stop and join together and pray for God's protection over the family member and for a safe return. Likewise, whenever any one of them would return home, the event was celebrated with another quick gathering to give a welcome and a prayer of thanks.

Richard was astonished at this family ritual, especially given there were five or six children and it was a busy household. What impressed him most, however, was the way the mother would gather all the children together to give their father a special welcome when he entered the home at the end of the day. It was not just a time of prayerful thanks; it was a joyful celebration!

Through this simple family tradition—a living metaphor for writing God's Word upon our doorposts and gates—they were living out the love they had for each other. They were also living out their recognition of the preciousness of each one in the family, as well as the precariousness of life in this world, such that we should never go anywhere apart from God's protection. The daily celebration of the father's homecoming was a continual reminder of the command to honor and to obey him in the Lord, as well as a visible testimony of the wife's reverence for and respect of her husband.

In our culture, teachable moments all too often teach anything but respect and honor, much less recognition of God's laws. Take for example, Laura George, the mother of a student in Loudoun County, Virginia, just outside Washington, D.C. When students started "freak dancing" at a high school dance, it caused a small stir, but not for the reasons you would think. True, chaperones left in disgust at the sight of boys standing behind girls simulating sexual intercourse, and the principal requested that students pledge not to bring drugs, alcohol, *or* engage in freak dancing at the next school dance. However, none of the parents asked that the dances be suspended. None asked the principal to discipline the offenders. None of the parents were known to have disciplined their own children.

No. Instead, when the students *protested* against the principal's "abridgement of their student rights" by requesting them to sign the pledge, the parents, including Laura George, supported their children. George stated, "Civil rights are falling by the wayside every second. I've got to take a stand here for my kids. I've got to teach them that you question authority when authority's gone mad."[12]

Modeling Mature Kingdom Discipleship

It's certain that both the culture in general, and many of today's parents, in particular, have a distorted view of what it means to nurture and train children, but are we sure that we have any better understanding inside our churches? Over the years, George Barna has discovered some unsettling facts about the state of churches in America. In 2000, Barna looked at the subject of *discipleship*. His research indicated that many Christians have a fuzzy notion of what it means to be a disciple of Jesus Christ.

Barna interviewed 417 Christians that he identified as "born again believers," based on their testimonies that they had made a personal commitment to Jesus Christ by repenting of their sins and accepting Him as their Savior.[13] He asked them to identify the chief source of success and meaning in their lives and found that the majority (8 out of 10) identified some dimension *other than* spirituality. Even among the small minority (2 out of 10) who identified a spiritual outcome as their "crowning achievement in life," that outcome was stated in very basic terms in half the cases. Respondents described it in terms of "knowing that they are saved" or "maintaining faith in God."[14]

If Barna's research is representative, it shows there is, indeed, a great need for teaching and training *within* the church in order to share and develop a vision of "what human life and community begin to look like when people come under the reign and rule of God," as Tullian Tchividjian, senior pastor of Coral Ridge Presbyterian Church, states it. Tchividjian points out that Jesus has given us just such a vision in Matthew 5:1-12. According to Tchividjian, Jesus' sermon should not be viewed as a list of "eight separate characteristics, as if Jesus were saying 'Some will be meek, others will be merciful, and still others will be peacemakers.' Rather, these are eight marks of character that, to a greater or lesser extent will be present in the lives of those to whom Jesus is King."[15]

Following Jesus, submitting ourselves to Him as our Lord, as our King, requires coming to know *who Jesus is,* and in Matthew 5, we see, first of all, a description of *"who Jesus is,"* says Tchividjian.

> [H]e is humble, he is gentle, he is merciful, he is pure in heart, and he is the ultimate peacemaker. If we have bowed the knee to King Jesus and have come under the reign and rule of his kingdom, we will increasingly "reflect the Lord's glory" as we "are being transformed into his likeness with ever-increasing glory, which comes from the Lord, who is the Spirit" (2 Corinthians 3:18 NIV). Because Jesus is like this, we are becoming more and more like this . . . we are, in short, *becoming* more and more like Christ. The kingdom of God is made up of citizens who are in *process.*[16]

What if those George Barna had interviewed had expressed this vision for *becoming more like Christ,* for growing spiritually, for developing a mature faith, for leaving behind adolescent spiritual ways, for growing in confidence and trust in Him, for casting aside idolatrous ideas of what He is like, for going to Scripture to learn of Him and to see Him more clearly, for reflecting more and more of His character? Isn't this what's needed today if the elder generations are to pass along to the coming generations the heritage of faith, as David speaks of in Psalm 78, verses 1-8?

Tell the Coming Generation
A Maskil of Asaph.

Give ear, O my people, to my law;
Incline your ears to the words of my mouth.

> *I will open my mouth in a parable;*
> *I will utter dark sayings of old,*
> *Which we have heard and known,*
> *And our fathers have told us.*
> *We will not hide them from their children,*
> *Telling to the generation to come the praises of the LORD,*
> *And His strength and His wonderful works that He has done.*
>
> *For He established a testimony in Jacob,*
> *And appointed a law in Israel,*
> *Which He commanded our fathers,*
> *That they should make them known to their children;*
> *That the generation to come might know them,*
> *The children who would be born,*
> *That they may arise and declare them to their children,*
> *That they may set their hope in God,*
> *And not forget the works of God,*
> *But keep His commandments;*
> *And may not be like their fathers,*
> *A stubborn and rebellious generation,*
> *A generation that did not set its heart aright,*
> *And whose spirit was not faithful to God.*

How can we expect our youths to grow into spiritual maturity if we ourselves are not providing them with strong examples of mature discipleship in our own lives?

John H. Westerhoff III shares some profound insights about this task of teaching the next generation in what he calls "Modeling the Adult Pilgrimage."

> If I have learned anything over the years, it is this:
> We need to make the religious aspects of our lives a

priority; we need to make our growth in faith our first commitment in terms of time and energy. Only then can we deal with our own anxiety, admit that we will never be the perfect parent, and acknowledge that our children are in God's hands. Then we can relax, and instead of trying to live for our children, we can live for ourselves and share ourselves with them. Only when we turn to our own faith and life do we have anything to share with our children. That is what this chapter is about; it is an invitation to work out our salvation, to continue the journey begun at our baptism, to engage ourselves seriously in the pilgrimage of faith so we might live faithfully with our children and thereby bring them up in the Christian faith.[17]

Parents and teachers who are growing in their own faith will have things to share with their children as they "sit in the house, walk by the way, lie down, and rise up." Every leave taking will be significant—every homecoming an event.

Chapter Seven

TOLERANCE: THE LAST VIRTUE

The earliest American schools were founded to advance the Christian faith.[1] New England Puritans passed laws providing for every community with 50 households to appoint a schoolmaster to teach children to read and write. The view, as expressed in a Connecticut law in 1655, was that:

> ... all their children, and apprentices as they grow capable, may through God's blessing, attain at least so much, as to be able duly to read the Scriptures and other good and profitable printed books in the English tongue, being their native language, and in some competent measure, to understand the main grounds and principles of Christian Religion necessary to salvation.[2]

This was the prevailing viewpoint for about the next 175 years. During the Founding Period of the American Revolution, leaders such as Benjamin Franklin, Samuel Adams, George Washington, and Gouverneur Morris spoke of the importance of education and the "religious principle" to the health and welfare of the new nation. As Sam Kastensmidt writes in *The Bible and the Blackboard*:

> Gouverneur Morris, the most active participant in the Constitutional Convention, proclaimed, "Religion is the only solid basis of good morals; therefore, education should teach the precepts of religion, and the duties of man towards God.[3]

How we wish today's legislators had the view of Samuel Adams, the "Father of the American Revolution" and a state senator and governor of Massachusetts. Adams believed that for America to "establish the permanent foundations of freedom and happiness," our nation's "divines and philosophers, statesmen and patriots," must:

> ... unite their efforts to renovate the age by impressing the minds of men with the importance of educating their little boys and girls, inculcating in the minds of youth the fear and love of the Deity.[4]

Thomas Jefferson, after noting American students who studied in England learned "drinking, horse racing, and boxing," and any student who studied in Europe acquired "a fondness for European luxury and dissipation, and a contempt for the simplicity of his own country," argued against sending America's youth to European universities. "Who are the men of most learning, of most eloquence, most beloved by their countrymen and most trusted and promoted by them?" he asked. "They are those who have been educated among them, and whose manners, morals, and habits are perfectly homogeneous with those of the country."[5]

This high priority placed on morals and on the Christian religion as the basis of any good morals, can hardly be imagined by today's educators, most of whom are taught that it was the common-school movement of Horace Mann that birthed American public education and shaped its destiny. "Most students today," points out educator Thomas Lickona, "are ignorant of the role of religion in our moral beginnings and development as a nation. One reason is that since the 1960s, the story of religion in American history has shrunk to nearly nothing in the public school textbooks."[6]

Writing in 1991, Lickona (who admired Thomas Aquinas and recognized the Holy Spirit as the source of all truth) tried valiantly to reintroduce "Education for Virtue" into public education. Nevertheless, the multicultural education movement of the 1990s swept onward and firmly entrenched moral relativism as the dominant framework for government controlled public school curriculums.

In explaining why American education moved away from the Founders' view that "Moral education … is essential for the success of a democratic society," Lickona attributes the change to the rise of Darwinism, the influence of Einstein's theory of relativity on thinking about moral behavior, empirical psychology's influence on educational theory, and the philosophy of logical positivism, which made a dichotomy between *facts* and *values*.[7] These influences, starting with Darwin's publication of *On the Origin of Species* in 1859, have built a towering wall of unbelief and humanism around American public schools—one that will brook no Christian intruders. According to Lickona, the capstone of "personalism" was placed on top the tower of unbelief during the turbulent '60s and '70s and the banner of "human freedom and personal fulfillment" unfurled.

Lickona's explanation has merit, but we also need to revisit the first half of the story: what took place in American education from 1830 to 1859. But before we look at the dramatic changes that started to reshape America's schools in the late 1830s, let's examine their roots in the Pilgrim and Puritan society of the early colonies.

The True Roots of American Education

The early consensus of the Pilgrims and Puritans on the importance of education remained in place for almost 200 years. Massachusetts Bay Colony enacted the first law in 1642 "requiring that families and masters teach children and apprentices how to read English 'perfectly,' provide them with knowledge of the capital laws of the colony, and instruct them in orthodox catechisms."[8] Other colonies followed suit, thus establishing a form of "universal education."

But, as Bruce Shortt points out in his excellent book, *The*

Harsh Truth About Public Schools, the ideal of universal education found among the colonies was really "a legacy of the Reformation," which had changed the attitude of the church about the education of the laity.[9] As Shortt explains,

> [a]lthough the [Roman] Catholic Church had often provided an exceptional education to its elite and had done much to preserve the learning of antiquity following the fall of the Roman Empire, prior to the Reformation, no religious importance was attributed to having a literate Christian laity. . . . If anything, literacy among the laity was seen as potentially dangerous because it could lead to questioning of the authority of Rome, particularly if that literacy permitted them to read the Bible.[10]

This view changed with the Reformation. According to Shortt, the pivotal change was a return to the biblical view of the individual Christian believer's relationship to God.

> In addition to recovering the Biblical doctrine that we are justified by faith alone, the Reformation also swept away the unbiblical belief that a church bureaucracy or priestly class is required as an intermediary between Man and God. Instead, Protestants asserted the priesthood of all believers and understood that Man's relationship to God is direct and personal. But if Man's relationship to God was personal, so, too, were the snares laid for him by Satan. The Bible, then, was both the Christian's key to understanding God's plan of salvation and his bulwark against evil. Yet, what use was a Bible to a

Christian who could not read?[11]

The idea of the priesthood of believers became a tenet of all the reformers. Gary De Mar points out, however, that the Puritan system of schools was, in fact, a copy of John Calvin's academy in Geneva. "The purpose of these colonial schools was to further the gospel of Christ in all disciplines."[12] Not only were America's first schools modeled after those of John Calvin,[13] two-thirds of America's 200 colleges at the time of the Civil War "were either founded or controlled by the theological heirs of John Calvin."[14]

John Calvin's Model for Education

So what was so distinctive about John Calvin's vision for education that the Puritans believed it should be the foundation for their schools? Why did it become the model for so many of America's colleges? According to Henry R. Van Til, who considered Calvin's contribution in the field of education in *The Calvinistic Concept of Culture,* Calvin's view was rooted in his understanding of the need for both *reformation of the church* and *renovation of the culture.*

One of Calvin's first concerns upon arriving in Geneva in 1536 was to set up both a school for the education of youth and an institution of higher learning. Although it was not until 1559 that a *collège* (Academy) was established, when Calvin died five years later, there were 1,200 students studying in its lower grammar school and 300 in the upper level *académie,* which became the University of Geneva. The impact of the Academy was felt throughout Europe, as the scholars who were trained there in theology, art, science, law, and medicine settled outside of Geneva.

In establishing the order for *du College de Geneva,* Calvin articulated his vision for education. As Van Til says,

From his *Ordre du College de Genève* it is clear that
the basic objective of education was the knowledge
of God and of his creation unto the service of God.
Such knowledge could be achieved by the study of
history, as represented in the classics, and nature, as
set forth in natural science. However, since the fall,
the natural man cannot come to the true knowledge
of God or of his world without regeneration, which
alone makes it possible to grasp the meaning of
God's revelation in Scripture, and restores man to
the proper perspective.[15]

What Calvin so clearly saw was that as Christians, we do not
just learn for the purpose of our own "personal fulfillment" or "self-
actualization," as is the view of contemporary educators. Rather,
Calvin understood that our learning must be for service: both
immediate, as in the teaching of others and in our professions, and
ultimate, as in the service of God and his kingdom. In elaborating on
this, Van Til wrote,

As a matter of fact, a liberal education [Note: Van
Til is using the term *liberal* in its classical sense, not
a political sense.] may not be divorced from man's
goal in life, namely understanding the Scriptures in
order to do the will of God. Liberal arts and sciences
do not give us the true knowledge of God, unless our
eyes have first been opened through the Spirit.[16]

Once our eyes have been opened, we can see the world with clear
vision. Now we are ready to embark on the path of *true education*—
which by definition must begin by acknowledging the God of
creation, who has created us to depend upon Him and His laws for

creation for our very subsistence and life. Apart from His grace, we can never know any spiritual truth concerning either His creation or ourselves.[17]

The Progressives' Hostile Takeover

This Calvinist vision for education was the model in New England for almost 200 years, until around 1840, when it began to be undermined right in the backyard of the early Puritans. Horace Mann, who, as every teacher education student must learn, is considered "The father of the common schools," was appointed Secretary in 1837 of the newly created Board of Education of Massachusetts. Using this position, he began to promote ideas about schooling and school "reform" that would spread across the entire nation. Even in faraway California, they embraced the ideals of the system of schooling which became known as the "common schools."

In spite of the fact that his early home church training had been in the "orthodox Calvinism of the day," Horace Mann was "a thorough believer in the doctrine of the 'perfectibility of man.'"[18] His religion, as R. J. Rushdoony points out in *The Messianic Character of American Education,* was "essentially moralism rather than piety." Mann, along with other Unitarians of his day, saw himself as a "legitimate heir" of the Puritans, just the same as those who still claimed to be Calvinists. Nevertheless, these two lines of descendents from the New England Puritans viewed their religious roots quite differently. Today, Calvinists still believe that Christianity is essentially a *salvation* religion; for Mann and his fellow Unitarians, it was essentially a *Libertarian* religion. In their view, "the Puritans broke with the past and its bondage to create a new and freer society…. This spirit of freedom was the essence of Christianity."[19]

Horace Mann's stated belief, "If God is our *Father,* all men must be our brethren," [20] became a foundational tenet for the ideology of the common-school movement, which was the first effort to bring all children in America into a "common" educational setting. In the teacher education textbook, *School and Society,* the purpose of the "public school" as it was being shaped by Mann is described:

> … it would attempt to create citizens committed to a secular faith whose moral values would play much the same role that doctrine had played in sectarian faith. In a figurative sense, the school would become the temple, the teacher the minister, and the school boards the temple elders. American schoolchildren would be taught a pan-Protestant brand of citizenship which would wed religion and nationalism…. The idea was not new, for this idea had energized earlier Puritan education…. What was new was the systemic government-supported scope of this approach. [21]

The authors of *School and Society* reveal their own bias in the sentence that follows: "It would take a series of painful U.S. Supreme Court decisions in the mid-twentieth century to eliminate religious references and rituals in schools, thus rectifying the Protestant precedent set by Mann in Massachusetts." [22] In reality, Mann left only a veneer of Protestantism. The heart and soul of true Calvinism had been eviscerated and replaced by a moralistic view of God as "the Father of us all."

Once these schools were established in communities all across the country, they began indoctrinating children into a set of "common values," such as Horace Mann's conception of the "fatherhood of God and the brotherhood of man." As prevalent as that notion is today, even among some Christians, it is far from biblical. In his chapter on

"Adoption" in *Truths That Transform*, D. James Kennedy wrote:

> The concept of the universal fatherhood of God
> and universal brotherhood of man is utterly
> foreign to Scriptures.... Paul says we were
> "children of disobedience" (Ephesians 2:2). This
> is the state of the natural man as he is born into
> this world. He is a disobedient child of the devil,
> under the wrath of God. One family with one
> Father? Not at all! We must be translated out of
> the kingdom of darkness into the kingdom of
> God's dear Son. All sons of God? Listen: "But as
> many as received him [Christ], to them gave he
> power to become the sons of God (John 1:12)."[23]

When Horace Mann received his political appointment with
the Massachusetts State Board of Education in the late 1830s,
he stepped onto a platform that he turned into a national bully
pulpit for what was just the first of many waves of reform that have
swept through America's schools. But what Mann accomplished
was more than reform—it was a *remaking* of schooling in
America. By setting in motion the movement for establishing a
system of universal, compulsory, publicly-funded education in the
states, he essentially overturned the intent of the Pilgrim and Puritan
founders. Their goal was that schools would enable children "to
understand the main grounds and principles of Christian Religion
necessary to salvation," as the Connecticut law of 1655 stated.

According to Rushdoony, it was Mann who laid the
groundwork for the rhetoric of today's educationists. Using his
bully pulpit, he argued that the common schools (not churches!)
were the primary social institution that could (and should) exert
both a "curative" and a "remedial" influence on society. Therefore,

using public funding to support schools was for the betterment of society. The refrain that we are so familiar with today—"Give us the money and we can do it; our failure thus far is your fault in that we have received insufficient funds," started with the common-school movement.[24]

Before moving on, one additional point must be made about the impact of the common-school movement. Common schools were promoted to Protestants as a means of assimilating the burgeoning number of Roman Catholics coming to America's shores due to the Great Famine of Ireland—hence the memorial to its *victims* now in Cambridge Common. Raging between 1845 and 1852, the potato famine caused the deaths of close to 25 percent of Ireland's population. It also sent tens of thousands to America on a quest for a better life.

Shortt explains that this caused consternation among American Protestants, who still vividly remembered "that their forebears had suffered terrible persecution in Europe at the hands of Catholics."[25] The promoters of the common schools won the support of Protestants for their public schools by telling them, "Nothing can Americanize these chaotic elements, and breathe into them the spirit of our institutions ... except the public schools."[26]

In hindsight, it's now clear that all the Protestants got for their cooperation was a "mess of pottage," which turned out to be much more than they had bargained for. The Progressives, such as Mann and many others, pushed to replace the various schools operating in America at that time—including academies for young men and young women, private Christian schools, and local schools—with *compulsory* public education for all children. By 1918, all the states had compulsory education laws on their books. These laws reflect the view of progressives that the state has the *right* to determine how children should be educated because, ultimately, human beings are "a form of collective property" of the state. Shortt provides a quote from John Swett, a California state superintendent of education during the 1860s, in which he made the stark claim: "[C]hildren arrived at the age of maturity belong, not to the parents, but to the State, to society, to the country."[27]

Swett's statement should have sent chills down the spine of every Christian parent of that day who was contemplating sending his child to the common schools. This is *still* the view of today's liberal-progressives, including Bill and Hillary Clinton. Furthermore, as we'll see in a subsequent chapter, then-Governor Clinton's educational reforms in Arkansas became the model for the federal level reforms mandated under George Bush Sr.'s administration.

Progressivism and Beyond

It is important to understand, as we've seen in the previous section, that the "progressive movement" in education did not start, as is often claimed, with John Dewey, the American philosopher and educational theorist. During his time, however, opponents of progressivism did arise, advocating for an "essentialist" philosophy of education for the public schools. Dewey accurately described this conflict as one between those who believed (as he did) that "education is development from within" versus those, such as the "essentialists," who believed that "it is formation from without." Dewey characterized this view of education as "a process of overcoming natural inclination and substituting in its place habits acquired under external pressure."[28]

This debate over the nature of education has raged among educational theorists from the very beginning—even the word *education* itself contributes to this conflict. It comes from the Latin verb *educare*, which is the combination of two words: the verb *ducare*—*to lead* or *to draw*, and the prefix *e*, which is a shortened form of *ex*—*out of* or *from*. If education is a "leading out," it requires, quite simply, someone to provide leadership, guidance, and even direction. If, on the other hand, as Dewey and his followers today believe, education is "a drawing out" of what is already inside the child, then the teacher is there only to assist the child in "constructing" knowledge. The teacher can't be the "sage on the stage," but must be the "guide on the side." This latter view is now so prevalent I've even encountered it in business training seminars.

These two contrasting views first showed up in the writings of Plato—hence their influence on educators ever since. In *The Meno*, Socrates' questioning *guides* an untutored slave to see the solution for a problem of geometry. The slave's insight is possible, according to Socrates, because he has "spontaneously recovered" some *innate knowledge* through a "recollection."[29] However, since this begs the question of where the "recollection" came from, contemporary theorists ignore the question of how we could have acquired such knowledge. Instead, they talk about all the ways children can be encouraged to *construct* knowledge for themselves.[30]

In one of his other dialogues, the *Republic*, Plato explains the nature of education differently. He provides the much-noted analogy of the cave. Inside the cave, children are strapped down to chairs. All they can see is the wall in front of them. From behind, a fire burns, causing the shadows of travelers moving along a road between the fire and the children to be cast on the wall. Even as they are growing up, the children only see the moving shadows on the wall. Therefore, as Socrates points out in the dialogue, even if as an adult "someone dragged him away from there by force along the rough, steep, upward way… out into the light of the sun," he would still "be distressed and annoyed at being so dragged," and it would take him some time to become accustomed to the light outside the cave.[31] In contrast to the *Meno*, this is not a picture of innate knowledge being gently drawn out of the learner by the teacher's careful questioning. Instead, the learner is dragged out into the sunlight where his eyes must adjust to the glaring light of truth.

Nevertheless, one essential feature is missing in both these examples. Nothing prevents either those in the cave or the slave from coming to the truth. In the one case, although blinded at first by the light once they left the cave, the eyes of Plato's cave dwellers were open, and their eyes later adjusted to the light. In the other case, nothing kept the untutored slave from discovering the truth within him, once Socrates arrived on the scene. Both these views, however, misrepresent our human relationship to knowledge and truth.

According to the biblical view, we are all sitting in darkness, without God and without hope, and our eyes are blinded by sin. We can't recognize the truth, even when we stand directly in front of it, unless the eyes of our hearts have been enlightened by Christ. Then, it is not to "know good and evil," but to know the desperate need we have for a Savior from our sin. Once saved from our sin, we can begin to know the glorious hope to which He has called us and the "immeasurable greatness of His power toward us who believe" (Ephesians 1:19).

Jesus' restoration of sight to the blind is something each and every one of us on this planet needs, if we are ever to come to a "knowledge of the truth." Before we can become Jesus' disciples, His followers, we must have our spiritual sight restored. Then, as we follow Him as one of His disciples, we can begin to learn—to be instructed by the Master Teacher. This learning process is also the process of our sanctification. Thus, to be truly educated, we must be *led* by the Savior.

Without this perspective, American educators have for years been following *false truths*, which are, in fact, idols constructed from the beliefs of their humanistic, man-centered worldview. These false ideas include—but are not limited to:

- *The perfectibility of man through education*
- *The religious neutrality of education*
- *The separation of educational facts from religious values*
- *The equality of all cultural values*
- *The belief that there are no moral absolutes*

Falsehoods such as these, as D. James Kennedy has pointed out, have led to the view that the only "sin" left in our society is that of "judging." Therefore, the supreme virtue we must teach is that of *tolerance.* The consequence of government-run, mandated schooling based on such beliefs is that in America today, as Dr. Kennedy said, "Many have joined that degenerate part of society for which there is only one 'virtue'—tolerance ... the last virtue of a totally degenerate society. For much of our society that is where we have arrived."[32]

Chapter Eight

THEY CLOSED DOWN THE MARKETPLACE OF IDEAS

Does regulating the Internet so service providers must give users opposing viewpoints on any topic seem outlandish? Does it seem laughable that people looking for arguments for the existence of God would be directed to sites that argue for atheism? Well, meet Cass Sunstein. Internet regulations like this are but one of his many ideas.

Sunstein, at the time of this writing, is still awaiting Senate approval as President Obama's "regulatory czar." In that role, he would head up the Office of Information and Regulatory Affairs. The OIRA is in charge of revising or rejecting all new rules proposed by all major federal agencies—such "rules" or mandates do not need to pass Congress, but they have the force of law nevertheless.

When discussing the possible need for regulation of the Internet, Sunstein argued that it is "anti-democratic," because it allows users to filter out information of their own choosing. This is yet another example of the now familiar form of verbal jujitsu that we see all too often in our political discourse—like calling an unplanned pregnancy an "unwanted pregnancy," or placing funding of abortions under the category of "reproductive health."

In this case, Sunstein probably knew he was on shaky ground, so he tried to justify his proposal by hedging it a bit: "A system of limitless individual choices, with respect to communications, is *not necessarily* [emphasis added] in the interest of citizenship and self-government."[1] We might agree with Sunstein *if* he had been talking about limitless access to pornography. But that was not his concern.

Closing down choices "with respect to communications" has been a favorite tactic of liberal-progressives for decades, especially when it comes to America's schools. As we'll see in this chapter, it's not just those who control curricula in government schools that have no patience with alternative viewpoints. The privileged class of the academic elites who dominate American universities mock and disparage anyone who does not follow their politically liberal and socially radical mindset.

Many Choices—But One Viewpoint

There is great irony in this. On the one hand, the number of courses across the curriculum has expanded enormously. North Carolina public schools offered more than 450 courses in 2000-2001. This already astonishing number grew to 500 in 2005-2006 with the addition of such courses as Afro-American Studies, Contemporary Issues in North Carolina, and Geography in Action.[2] But, while the variety of courses students can choose from has exploded, as Judge Robert Bork points out, these curricula share a common ideology: the politics of "race, class, and gender."[3]

Courses such as these place students into the politically correct world of "identity politics" and suit them up for the culture war on individual liberty and freedom. Long gone are general education classes of a few generations ago such as, "A Survey of Western Civilization" or "The Intellectual Foundations of the American Revolution," or, much less, "Reformation Europe and Its Influence in America."

Judge Bork's insight that *radical egalitarianism* is one of the ideologies driving our culture is evidenced by the current administration's efforts to "remake" American society.[4] Every sector—not just schooling—is now being pushed into a "one size fits all curriculum." In the economic realm, banks were forced to take TARP funds they didn't want or need; in the car industry, government regulations will soon determine which kinds of cars all manufacturers will be allowed/required to make; in health care, we may yet be forced into a "one size fits all" government health plan. We are even going to be required to use the correct kind of government mandated light bulbs.

"One size fits all" has been the enforced dogma in schooling for decades. "Tracking" is considered discriminatory, so academically talented students must be placed in classes with students who are several grades below in their reading level. Special needs students must be "mainstreamed" into regular classrooms, where regular classroom teachers struggle to give them the special attention they need, without neglecting other students.

Classical curriculums of the past, which were perceived as "elitist," have been tossed out to make way for more egalitarian courses that focus on local, community, or regional concerns of diverse ethnic and social groups—such as feminists and homosexuals. According to Judge Bork, by getting rid of general education requirements rooted in a classical view of learning, we are now "producing students who have information about narrow corners of subjects, but no conception of the larger context that alone can give the niches meaning."[5]

Reducing the curriculum to "narrow corners of subjects" limits students' horizons of knowledge and understanding. Their interests have become localized and limited to the personal and the mundane. Mark Bauerlein describes it this way:

> It isn't enough to say that these young people are uninterested in world realities. They are actively cut off from them. Or a better way to put it is to say that they are encased in more immediate realities that shut out conditions beyond— friends, work, clothes, cars, pop music, sitcoms, Facebook. Each day, the information they receive and the interactions they have must be so local or superficial that the facts of government, foreign and domestic affairs, the historical past, and the fine arts never slip through. How do they do it? Sounds hard, especially in an age of so much

information, so many screens and streams in private and public places.[6]

Not surprisingly, Bauerlein has titled his book from which this is quoted, *The Dumbest Generation: How the Digital Age Stupefies Young Americans and Jeopardizes Our Future (or Don't Trust Anyone Under 30)*. He has marshaled an enormous amount of evidence to support his contention that today's youth are clueless when it comes to the culture beyond their immediate realm of experience. One young reviewer, however, who identified himself as "part of the so-called 'dumbest generation,'" commented quite insightfully:

> That they [today's youth] have this attitude is not entirely their fault, since many of them attended schools where climbing out of the ignorance that all of us are born into was considered optional, lack of effort was no bar to moving up through the grades, and academic rigor was thought of as a cruel imposition on their innocent lives of play or perhaps (horrors) "elitist." Their peer environment was little help, as it punished those with a taste for academic work by calling them "nerds" or simply ignoring them.[7]

One has the sense that the reviewer's final observation is autobiographical.

Not Dumb—Disconnected

Josh McDowell says this is not the "dumbest" but the "disconnected generation." His concern is that "our kids today are disconnected from most adults and lack a sense of personal identity and purpose. Alienation from adults and fuzzy sense of identity cause them to feel adrift in a hostile world."[8] In McDowell's view, the very fact that today's kids can connect with friends so easily through use of technologies may mean that they are more likely to be disconnected relationally from their parents at home. "And since many homes are also equipped with PCs for Mom and Dad, kids and their parents spend more time staring at their monitors than they do interacting with one another," McDowell says.[9]

He made this observation in his book, *The Disconnected Generation*, published in 2000, before the more recent forms of social networking, such as MySpace, Facebook, Twitter, and texting. Unless parents have been making the kind of concerted efforts to connect with their kids that McDowell recommends in his book, it's quite possible the situation isn't much better nine years later. McDowell, however, is using every means possible to reach young people, who can now follow Josh on Twitter or contact him through Facebook.

George Barna's research on teens and twenty somethings confirms McDowell's view that it's essential for parents *and* the local church to connect with this age group. In *Boiling Point: Monitoring Cultural Shifts in the 21st Century*, Barna and Mark Hatch call attention to the characteristics of the *millennial* (or as Barna calls them, the *mosaic*) generation. They note that members of this generation have no interest in religious institutions *per se*, but attend church to develop friendships, and they view faith as "more about relationships than beliefs and rituals."[10]

Research by David Kinnaman on the use of technology among the generations also shows this primary concern for connectedness among youth. Whereas older adults use technology primarily for information and convenience, younger adults are using it to connect with friends. The new technologies, in particular, are "rewiring" the way young people "meet, express themselves, use content and stay connected."[11]

If parents are not connecting with their children, it's also likely they are not modeling kingdom discipleship and the pilgrimage of faith—educating them both *covenantally* and *culturally*. Nevertheless, even if parents do stay connected with their kids through the tumultuous times of adolescence, they may not realize that by sending their son or daughter off to a secular university, or even the local community college, they greatly increase the chance that their child will disconnect from their church and faith community. The radical Left's takeover of higher education has been well-documented, if largely ignored by Christians. The majority still send their youth to secular schools without first giving them a thorough grounding in how to critique and analyze worldviews that compete with Christianity.[12]

The number of Christian young people who renounce their faith before graduating from college is estimated at between 30 to 50 percent by Gary Railsback, based on the research he did for his doctoral degree in 1994.[13] Research by the Barna Group confirms this trend. Barna reported in 2006 that "twentysomethings continue to be the most spiritually independent and resistant age group in America. Most of them pull away from participation and engagement in Christian churches, particularly during the 'college years.'" Barna's researchers found that the number of young adults who had been involved in church life at one point in their teens but now were "spiritually disengaged," (i.e., not actively attending church, reading the Bible, or praying), was 61 percent—a number even higher than Railsback's.[14]

Also significant are the changes taking place with each successive generation in regard to the "no-faith segment" of each group. Whereas nine percent of Boomers consider themselves atheists or agnostics, and 14 percent of Gen Xers do, that number is 19 percent of Millenials. Furthermore, these numbers are not a reflection of generations becoming "more faith-oriented as they age," but have stayed relatively constant with each group over time.[15]

Radicals at the Door

According to both Robert Bork and Allan Bloom, the students who radicalized the universities during the '60s became the professors of the '70s, '80s, and '90s.[16] As former leftist David Horowitz says, "The cultural upheavals of that era saw the accession to academic tenure of a generation of activists who regarded the university as a platform from which to advance their political mission."[17] As the "radical son" of Communist Party members himself, David watched his parents go off to party meetings four or five times a week until 1956, when they learned the truth about Stalin's murderous regime from a report published in *The New York Times*. The *Times* reported on a secret speech by Nikita Khrushchev acknowledging the crimes Stalin had committed. After that, Horowitz's parents ceased any further political activities, but still "tried to remain true to their ideals" as Communists.

As a young radical leftist, Horowitz was deeply involved in the movement during the '60s, until he finally acknowledged the Left's double standards. While they rallied around causes that conformed to their ideological condemnation of capitalism, such as the leftist takeover of Nicaragua, they ignored those that didn't, such as the Communist holocaust in Cambodia.[18] Horowitz astutely discerned the religious roots of the Left:

> The idea that men can be as gods and re-create a paradise on earth is the serpentine promise of the Left. It is an idolatry that overshadows all others. When men put on the mantle of gods and attempt to remake the world in their own image, the results are hideous and destructive beyond conception.[19]

The radical Left's campaign to sideline, to suppress, and ultimately to silence opposing points of view in the classroom and the culture has always been a strategic part of their plan to remake society in their own image. Among the ideological godfathers of the '60s radicals were the European Marxist Herbert Marcuse, Italian Communist Party founder Antonio Gramsci, and Brazilian educational theorist Paulo Freire. David Horowitz explains that

> ... the radicals viewed universities as "means of cultural production" analogous to the "means of production" in Marx's revolutionary *schema*. To these professorial activists, the academic classroom offered a potential fulcrum for revolutionary change. Because the university trained journalists and editors, lawyers and judges, future political candidates and operatives, it provided a path to cultural "hegemony" and an opportunity to promote a radical transformation of the society at large.[20]

Central to achieving that transformation was the goal of freeing the university from any societal constraints that would impede their cause. As Gramsci had written:

> Everything must be done in the name of man's dignity and rights, and in the name of his autonomy and freedom from outside constraint. From the claims and constraints of Christianity, above all.[21]

A Higher Law—A "Superior" Morality

This cry for "autonomy and freedom from outside constraint" developed into a *radical individualism*, which Judge Robert Bork points out was the other ruling ideology of the '60s radicals. In practice, it was always in tension with *radical egalitarianism,* since the individual who seeks his own autonomy above all must exert it at the expense of the rights of others. Yet the radical leftists failed to see this tension, and they pursued their individual freedom of expression by indulging in a variety of hedonistic practices. This meant that the moral claims and constraints of Christianity had to be discredited, while they claimed for themselves a superior morality. Speaking of this, David Horowitz writes, "Like all radicals, we were intoxicated by our own virtue."[22]

Judge Bork notes with great insight, "Modern liberalism tends to classify all moral distinctions it does not accept as hateful and invalid."[23] We see this liberal mindset in action when Christians are bashed and castigated by the media and the press for standing up for Christian principles of marriage and life. During the '60s, the radical students who wanted to live as they pleased, unfettered by the outdated notion of *in loco parentis* on the college campus, justified their hedonism by declaring all moral constraints against them "invalid." What were the virtues of the radical leftists? Certainly not self-sacrifice—nor as Allan Bloom concluded, the morality of duty. "Somehow it was never the everyday business of obeying the law that was interesting; more so was breaking it in the name of the higher law."[24]

Bloom saw the consequence of this viewpoint firsthand as a professor at Cornell University, where, in April 1969, "ten thousand triumphant students" rallied in support of a group of black students who had "persuaded" the faculty "to do their will by threatening the use of firearms as well as threatening the lives of individual professors."[25] In his book *The Closing of the American Mind,* Bloom sorted through both the causes and the consequences of the radicals' takeover of Cornell and other universities. The "higher law" that the radicals appealed to was not new. It was, as Bloom notes, derived from "the leading notions of modern democratic thought," such as equality, freedom, peace, and cosmopolitanism.

But these notions were "absolutized and radicalized," and consequently there could be no balancing of these ideals, no tempering of them, and no recognition that in practice they may come into conflict with each other. Nor was there any willingness to recognize, as Bloom noted, that there would certainly be "natural differences in gifts or in habitual practice of the virtues, the restraints liberty must impose on itself."[26]

As a classical scholar and political philosopher, Allan Bloom had a unique perspective and insight regarding the "superiority" he found among the students in the '60s. "In addition to the desire to live as they pleased, a covert elitism was at work among them," he wrote, observing:

> A permanent feature of democracy, always and everywhere, is a tendency to suppress the claims of any kind of superiority, conventional or natural, essentially by denying that there is superiority, particularly with respect to ruling. The Platonic dialogues are full of young men who passionately desire political glory and believe they have the talent to rule. Plato admits that he himself was once such a young man. And they lived in a city where their peculiar right to rule was denied them, where they would find it difficult to get ruling office, and to do so they would have to make themselves into what the people wanted. They burned with that special indignation a man reserves for wrongs done to himself and believed that their potential could not be fulfilled in democratic Athens. They constituted a subversive group in the city, unfriendly to the

maintenance of its regime.[27]

Bloom found these same characteristics among the subversive young radicals who took over the campus of Cornell in the late '60s.

The Trickle-Down Effect

Such were the subversives of the 1960s and such are their heirs today. The "covert elitism" Bloom noted is still present. The heirs of the '60s radicals claim to have "gifts" which grant them special privileges and the right to rule without any of the titles to rule of wisdom, age, money, power, or even experience. By their rhetoric, they woo the masses and enthrall the generations whose education has left them bereft of any analytical tools to evaluate their preposterous claims. Firmly convinced of their own superior ability to rule, the new elite revel in the political power and glory that comes their way when they achieve it.

We see many such men and women on our nation's political scene today. And they thrive in the academy, along with the holdover radicals from the '60s, who, with thinning hair, ponytails and reading glasses, still wear their uniforms—Communist red star T-shirts and rainbow armbands. Their goal—to influence another generation of unsuspecting youth.

Considering that the writing of educational theorist Paulo Freire was mother's milk to the '60s radicals, it's not surprising to find some of them now ensconced as professors in schools of education across the country. Freire's book, *Pedagogy of the Oppressed*, is required reading at 14 out of the top 16 of these schools.[28] Among these professors is President Obama's friend, Bill Ayers. Son of a wealthy Chicago CEO and philanthropist, he became a leader of the radical Weather Underground, and "participated in the bombings of New York City Police

Headquarters in 1970, the United States Capitol building in 1971, and The Pentagon in 1972, as he noted in his 2001 book, *Fugitive Days*."[29]

Ayers was drawn to teaching in a small preschool at the same time his political views were being radicalized. Working for the Radical Education Project in 1968, he wrote *Education: An American Problem*. After his political activism in the '70s, Ayers apparently thought he had learned how to fix this problem. He went to Columbia University Teachers College to earn an Ed.D. in Curriculum and Instruction, and in 1987 he joined the faculty of the College of Education at the University of Illinois at Chicago. He now holds the "titles to rule" of Distinguished Professor of Education and Senior University Scholar. Likewise, Ayer's wife Bernardine Dohrn, also a former domestic terrorist, holds the positions as Associate Professor of Law at Northwestern University School of Law and Director of Northwestern's Children and Family Justice Center.

Among his "scholarly works," Ayers lists his memoir, *Fugitive Days*, which opens with a sentence ending in an obscene expletive. It is described by one reviewer as an "unapologetic memoir about his ten years in the Weather Underground."[30] In spring of 2008, even as he was gaining notoriety through his association in the 1990s with then candidate Barack Obama, Ayers was elected Vice President for the Curriculum Division of the 25,000 member American Educational Research Association. The AERA is the nation's largest organization of education-school professors and researchers. As columnist Sol Stern points out, "Ayers won the election handily, and there is no doubt that his fellow education professors knew whom they were voting for. In the short biographical statement distributed to prospective voters beforehand, Ayers listed among his scholarly books *Fugitive Days*."[31]

The easy forgiveness of Ayers' Weather Underground past and

his ready acceptance into the world of the academic elite, testifies to the influence of left-wing ideology in teacher education. Sol Stern described it in an article for the Manhattan Institute:

> Indeed, the education department at the University of Illinois is a hotbed for the radical education professoriate. As Ayers puts it in one of his course descriptions, prospective K–12 teachers need to "be aware of the social and moral universe we inhabit and ... be a teacher capable of hope and struggle, outrage and action, a teacher teaching for social justice and liberation." Ayers's texts on the imperative of social-justice teaching are among the most popular works in the syllabi of the nation's ed schools and teacher-training institutes. One of Ayers's major themes is that the American public school system is nothing but a reflection of capitalist hegemony. Thus, the mission of all progressive teachers is to take back the classrooms and turn them into laboratories of revolutionary change.[32]

If you didn't know that your child's classroom is now a "laboratory for revolutionary change," then you haven't read the textbooks that your child's teacher had to read to pass his or her teacher education classes in college. Although Barack Obama and the press following him referred to Bill Ayers as "a professor of English," Ayers hasn't been giving esoteric lectures on "Male Friendship from Aristotle to Almodovar" to a few hundred liberal arts students over the past 20 years. Rather, he's been solving "America's problem" by indoctrinating future K-12 teachers and lecturing on "education reform" at Florida State University and other institutions all across the country as a "Distinguished Professor of Education."[33]

Using the Classroom for Intellectual Repression, Not Inquiry

In his 1996 book, *Slouching Towards Gomorrah*, Judge Robert Bork described numerous examples of political correctness that he saw taking over higher education at that time. "It is impossible to imagine that academic inquiry flourishes where thought police abound," he wrote. "Indeed, the intellectual apparatus of the sixties radicals now dominating the universities is built for intellectual repression and not for inquiry."[34] The situation has not improved since then. Rather, it has become so notable that it has spawned a new genre of *academic exposés*. Mike S. Adams, a professor of criminal justice at the University of North Carolina-Wilmington, has written *Welcome to the Ivory Tower of Babel: Confessions of a Conservative College Professor,* recounting the effects of the politically correct "diversity movement" on campuses, where students and professors are restricted by "speech codes" lest they give offense to any groups that now hold privileged positions on campus. These groups include homosexuals and feminists—but not Christians, who can be offended with impunity.[35]

Ben Shapiro has described his experiences as a student at UCLA in *Brainwashed: How Universities Indoctrinate America's Youth.* As Shapiro points out, the academy has always challenged the prevailing authority structures of the day. Thus, in modern-day universities, "Where the society preaches morality, the universities rebel against morality. Where the society embraces capitalism, the universities challenge capitalism. Where the society supports America, the universities disparage it."[36]

From a student perspective, however, Shapiro claims that students are ill-equipped because of their youthful naïveté and their lack of analytical skills and knowledge to resist indoctrination by their professors. Furthermore, he notes:

> Professors capitalize on the profound respect
> students feel for them. By telling students "think
> for yourselves" and "don't buy what your parents
> tell you," the professors set themselves up as the
> final authority on morality, politics, and society
> by discarding parents as moral arbiters. And
> students buy into it because they are always
> rebelling against their parents—and in college,
> this is a sanctioned and blessed activity.[37]

In *One Party Classroom*, David Horowitz describes dozens of college courses where radical indoctrination is taking place. In his book, *The Professors: The 101 Most Dangerous Academics in America,* Horowitz profiles some of the most radical professors teaching these courses, including Bill Ayers and Sami (Osama) Al-Arian, who taught engineering at the University of South Florida before finally being arrested for terrorist activities as the North American head of the Palestinian Islamic Jihad.

One of the most troubling aspects of the radicals' takeover of college and university campuses across our country, according to Horowitz, is that professors routinely have been using "their classroom to voice their nonprofessional, and often passionately expressed opinions on the war in Iraq and other matters that were irrelevant to the subjects they taught and outside of their areas of expertise." In hundreds of interviews of students across campuses, he "rarely encountered a student who had not been subjected to such in-class abuse."[38]

If one wonders why academics have been so opposed to the Iraq war, Horowitz gives an explanation in *Unholy Alliance: Radical Islam and the American Left.* Since radical leftists look at the world through the red-tinted lens of Marxism, which divides the world into "oppressors" and "oppressed," capitalism is considered the root cause of *all global* problems. Therefore America, as "the system's guardian-in-chief," must be undermined in everything she does; her wars must be opposed, as well as her peace.[39]

Horowitz is attempting to pry open the marketplace of ideas in higher education by proposing that a new Academic Bill of Rights be accepted by university systems and the American Association of University Professors—and even state legislatures.[40] He has also established a student organization, Students for Academic Freedom, which now has chapters on campuses around the country. He concludes his book *Indoctrination U* with the recommendation that "new departments" need to be established within the universities in order to "invigorate a marketplace of ideas that has experienced a dramatic constriction during the decades of political correctness and the regime of radical discourse." The agendas of such departments, he says, should be "to study free institutions, not to praise or denigrate them."[41]

Nevertheless, such efforts are slow moving. Meanwhile, the Alliance Defense Fund's Center for Academic Freedom continues to litigate cases on behalf of Christian students and professors whose freedom of speech has been curtailed on their campuses for voicing or defending a Christian point of view.[42]

A Kingdom View of Higher Education

What should Christian parents consider when deciding where to send their children to college? Higher education should be *liberal,* not as in its contemporary meaning—*favorable to progress or reform,* but as in the meaning of its Latin root *liber—free, independent, unrestrained.* Students should find higher education "freeing" in the sense that John Calvin affirmed its role. Once our eyes have been opened by the Holy Spirit, all the wonders of creation testify to our hearts and minds of God's governance of the universe through all the structures of space and time.

Christian philosopher and theologian Cornelius Van Til expressed this liberating power of education for the Christian in an essay, "Creation: The Education of Man—A Divinely Ordained Need:"

> What, then, do we mean by education? *Education is implication into God's interpretation.* No narrow intellectualism is implied in this definition. To think God's thoughts after Him, to dedicate the universe to its Maker, and to be the vice-gerent of the Ruler of all things: this is man's task. Man is prophet, priest, and king. It is this view of education that is involved in and demanded by the idea of creation.[43]

Van Til sees within creation "a divine ordinance for education" that can only be carried out in its fullness by those who hold to a Christian-theistic philosophy of education.

For those Christian students then, who are not being challenged "to think God's thoughts after Him" by Christian professors at a Christian college, the least their parents can do is prepare them to face the *liberal-progressive-radical* views of non-Christian professors by fully equipping them with the analytical tools and knowledge available to them by means of Christian worldview training.[44] Perhaps then we will "stop the bleeding" of the youths who are leaving the church. The sober fact is, as *USA Today* reported using data from a 2007 survey done by LifeWay Research:

Seven in 10 Protestants ages 18 to 30—both

evangelical and mainline—who went to church regularly in high school said they quit attending by age 23, according to the survey by LifeWay Research. And 34% of those said they had not returned, even sporadically, by age 30. That means about one in four Protestant young people have left the church.[45]

Chapter Nine

VIRTUOUS CITIZENS OR WORKERS OF THE WORLD?

W hat should students look like after twelve years of education in American schools? Should they be "agents for social change"—à la radical Bill Ayers? Should they be on the road to "maximizing their full human potential"—as per humanist psychologist Abraham Maslow? Or should they be "democratic citizens" who are continuously "reconstructing" their experience, since, as John Dewey claimed, "the process and goal of education are one and the same thing."[1]

The United Nations 1948 Declaration of Human Rights claims that "Everyone has the right to education," and sets forth this goal:

> Education shall be directed to the full development of the human personality and to the strengthening of respect for human rights and fundamental mental freedoms. It shall promote understanding, tolerance and friendship among all nations, racial or religious groups, and shall further the activities of the United Nations for the maintenance of peace.[2]

Most Americans would still take issue with that view. But the fact is that as far as government controlled public schools are concerned, neither you, nor I, nor most parents, nor even local school board members, have had much say in determining what the educational goals of public schools should be since 1989. In fact, America's government schools are now closer to having their goals determined by the UN than they are by local school boards.

It started with President George H. W. Bush, who worked with the nation's governors on a set of goals for educational reform. The result was called AMERICA 2000. President Bill Clinton essentially took *these same goals* for his education reform agenda and cast them as Goals 2000.[3] In spring of 1994, Congress passed three bills setting up the mandates. The funding bill HR6 was the strong arm that forced all the states to go along with Goals 2000 or lose federal funding—about seven percent of their total K-12 expenditures.[4] President George W. Bush's No Child Left Behind Act of 2001 had the same coercive provision to ensure compliance. Also, NCLB *didn't change the goals*: it just put in place an accountability plan to ensure that states would work more assiduously on them.

Where did the elder Bush and the governors get their goals? It gets a little murky trying to find the original objectives crafted by the governors. The process was started, however, under the direction of then-Gov. Bill Clinton of Arkansas, who chaired the National Governors Association from 1986 to 1987. Clinton was already making a name for himself nationally as the "Education Governor" because of reforms in his state—many of them under the guidance of his wife Hillary.

But starting with Bush Sr.'s AMERICA 2000, these goals have all lined up with a declaration adopted in 1990 by representatives from 155 countries and 150 non-governmental organizations (NGOs) at a UN-sponsored summit. Because George the First signed The World Declaration on Education for All (EFA) as a representative of the United States, it now functions as "soft law" in the U.S. As such, it has shaped federal educational policies of every administration since then. Like all international "declarations," "protocols," and "agreements," once signed by the executive branch, such a declaration functions as federal policy without ever having to cross the desk of a single U.S. senator or congressman.[5] Since President George H. W. Bush signed us on, the action plan and timeline prescribed by the World Declaration on Education for All, has been diligently followed by subsequent administrations.[6]

Say What?

If this is news to you, it certainly was to me when I first learned of the connection between the UN backed EFA and the Bush/ Clinton Goals 2000, as well as George W.'s No Child Left Behind. Most of the texts I used as a teacher-educator in the mid-1990s went into more detail about the Education for All Handicapped Children Act, passed in 1975, than they did the newly passed Goals 2000 measures. Even the extensive discussion I found in a standard text for educational foundations, *American Education*,[7] which gives an excellent overview of the Clinton "human capital agenda," does not contain a whiff of the connection between federal education goals and the U.N.'s Education for All declaration embraced by most of the nations of the world.

All one has to do, however, is to compare the two to see that Goals 2000 measures up remarkably close to the EFA requirements that President Bush Sr. signed.[8] A little further digging turns up connections between the non-governmental organizations (NGOs) working to implement EFA goals and other NGOs that are getting government grants to operate "programs in collaboration with policy leaders" (such as the federal Department of Education) and to provide "technical assistance" to help states comply with the requirements of the federal law.[9] Additionally, the United States submits an annual report to UNESCO (United Nations Education, Scientific and Cultural Organization) on progress implementing the EFA goals. When the World Education Forum met in April 2000 to update an action plan and revise the timeline for the EFA, President Bill Clinton signed it, and right on schedule, President George W. Bush proposed the No Child Left Behind Act of 2001, which fulfilled the requirements of the new timeline.[10]

While President George H. W. Bush's signing of the EFA was omitted, one topic that got a lot of coverage in my teacher education texts was *national standards*. As Diane Ravitch points out in her book, *National Standards in Education: A Citizen's Guide*, the agreement between President Bush Sr. and the governors to establish a set of goals for America's schools, set in motion the movement for *national standards*.[11] Feared by some and lauded by others, the system of comprehensive subject matter standards mandated by Goals 2000 has been the Trojan horse for what in effect is a *national curriculum*.[12]

Ratchet forward to 2009. Secretary of Education Arne Duncan, a Chicago basketball buddy of Barack Obama, is charging forward with the plan to develop "internationally benchmarked" national standards. Speaking at the American Council on Education (ACE) annual meeting in February, Duncan asserted that, "Taken together— the Barack effect, the leadership on the Hill, the proven strategies, and the money in the stimulus package—represent what I call the perfect storm for reform, a historic alignment of interests and events that could lift American education to an entirely new level."

Duncan's "Barack effect" is what he calls, "the soft power that accompanies the symbolism of an African-American president who has made education cool and exciting and infinitely promising.... Barack and Michelle Obama can be those role models on a national scale."[13]

Duncan wants more than role models in the White House, however. Now is the time, in his view, to move forward with a uniform system of curricular standards, as he explained to his audience of college and university administrators at the ACE meeting:

> We have to start by recognizing that our system of education is not aligned. Every state has different high school standards. If we accomplish one thing in the coming years—it should be to eliminate the

extreme variation in standards across America. I know that talking about standards can make people nervous—but the notion that we have fifty different goalposts is absolutely ridiculous. A high school diploma needs to mean something— no matter where it's from. We need standards that are college-ready and career-ready, and benchmarked against challenging international standards. We also need to break the culture of blame in which colleges blame high schools and high schools blame grade schools and grade schools blame parents for our failures. We are all part of one system of learning that begins at birth and never stops.[14]

So, while President Obama is carrying out his plan to "remake" America, his Secretary of Education sees a "perfect storm" opportunity for reforming American education so that we can all be "part of one system of learning that begins at birth and never stops."

But what about those of us who don't want to be a part of "one system?" Germany, which appears not to have learned any lessons in this area from its Nazi past, has made homeschooling illegal, thus negating parents' rights to educate their own children according to their moral convictions.[15] Great Britain now requires homeschoolers to "register" their children."[16] But Arne Duncan's got a triple whammy plan: 1) impose a "one size fits all" set of national standards across all the states, 2) benchmark our national standards against international standards, and 3) make us all "part of one system of learning that begins at birth and never stops."

His statements should have provoked a strong reaction from state education policymakers as well as Christian educators. If they did, the mainstream media didn't cover it. Having heard Secretary Duncan's announcement of his plan, however, we should all be on high alert. We should be paying close attention to what comes out of the federal Department of Education and this administration during the next four years.

What's the Problem With National Standards?

It might seem that requiring students to achieve certain levels of academic competence and measuring their performance against a set of national standards is harmless enough. Surely there's no "conspiracy" here. Don't we all want America's students to look good when compared to the students of other nations? Shouldn't we be in favor of such measures as the National Assessment of Educational Progress (NAEP), which the Education Department wants all the states to use so their students can be compared with students in other states, and ultimately with those in other nations? Isn't it a good idea to have a set of *national standards* as well as a means of testing all students to ascertain whether they have actually learned the content determined by these standards?

Professor Allen Quist worked to legalize homeschooling in Minnesota as a state legislator and now teaches political science at Bethany Lutheran College in Minnesota. He explained why a national curriculum is dangerous in his book, *FedEd: The New Federal Curriculum and How It's Enforced*. The problem, in one word, is *control*. Curriculum is what drives education, standards are what drive curriculum, and if we have a set of national standards— determined by the federal government—we will have schools that are doing the bidding of the federal government, not the local school boards and parents who elect them.

As noted above, Goals 2000 had a "human capital agenda," according to the textbook, *American Education*. The Clinton administration set in motion a plan for "life-long learning" in order to improve the skills of the nation's workforce, with the ultimate goal of preparing "workers for global corporations and for competition in a world labor market."[17] As Quist points out, however, this "reform" effort was, in fact, a "restructuring" of American education that handed over political control of America's schools to the federal government—without complaint by the citizenry, except for a few educators who questioned the legitimacy of schooling for the purpose of developing "human capital for a world economy."

Loss of Local Control

The first educational reform movement in America, the common-school movement of Horace Mann, had a profound impact by changing the moral content and context of schooling. Protestant churches supported the common schools in large part because they feared that the incoming mass of Roman Catholic immigrants would not be "Americanized" or integrated into American society unless they were forced to attend these common schools. In *The Public Orphanage: How Public Schools Are Making Parents Irrelevant*, Eric Buehrer gives some additional reasons why this movement was so significant:

> Opponents held that state-run education posed a basic threat to liberty, that compulsory-education laws were immoral, and that an "approved" curriculum would amount to indoctrination in government-endorsed views.[18]

From the beginning, those who opposed establishing state-run schools feared an "approved" curriculum—and with good reason. They saw then that it would take away parent's rights and liberties to teach their children in accordance with their own religious beliefs and values. They also feared "compulsory" education, seeing it as "immoral." Today the liberal-progressive view is that it is immoral *not* to provide universal public education since, as the UN Declaration on Human Rights states in Article 26, "Everyone has the right to education." Furthermore, according to the UN, "Education shall be free, at least in the elementary and fundamental stages. Elementary education shall be compulsory."[19]

The common-school movement in the 1840s and '50s was successful in introducing compulsory education to American schooling. In 1852, Massachusetts became the first state to pass compulsory school attendance laws.[20] Now all states have laws that penalize parents who do not send their children to school. According to school law expert Dr. Martha M. McCarthy:

> The legal basis for compulsory education is grounded in the common law doctrine of *parens patriae* which means that the state, in its guardian role, has the authority to enact reasonable laws for the well-being of its citizens. An enlightened citizenry is considered necessary to ensure the well-being of the state, and the individual has a legal obligation to give up a measure of personal freedom in the interest of the state's welfare.[21]

In 1922, with the support of the Grand Masonic Lodge, the Ku Klux Klan, and Democrat Gov. Walter M. Pierce, Oregon citizens passed a referendum requiring all students to attend Oregon public schools. Oregon's Compulsory Education Act was a direct effort to shut down all Catholic parochial schools in the state, but even before it went into effect, the U.S. Supreme Court ruled against it in *Pierce v. Society of Sisters* (1925). *Pierce* established the right of parents to send their children to private schools to comply with compulsory attendance laws, and as McCarthy notes:

The Court concluded that by restricting attendance to public institutions, the state interfered with private schools' rights to exist and with parents' rights to govern the upbringing of their children. The Court recognized that "the fundamental theory of liberty upon which all governments in this union repose excludes any general power of the state to standardize its children by forcing them to accept instruction from public teachers only." In essence, parents do not have the right to determine *whether* their children are educated, but they do have some control over *where* such education takes place.[22]

As of 1999–2000, approximately 27,000 private schools accounted for 24 percent of all schools in the U.S. and 12 percent of all full-time-equivalent teachers.[23] When McCarthy wrote in 1987, 85 percent of private schools in America were church related. That number appears to have remained fairly stable since then.[24]

Whether schools are for the purpose of developing "human capital for a global economy" or for "preserving the social order," supporters of public schools continue to claim that they are necessary "to prevent and reduce poverty and crime, provide better workers for business and industry, reduce tensions between social classes, assimilate immigrants, and prepare citizens to exercise their right to vote."[25]

The great contradiction in public school governance, however, is that although they are deemed necessary for "the common good" of society, they are not under the control of those members of society that they purportedly serve. Control of public schools has been steadily shifting out of the hands of local school boards who are accountable to parents, into the hands of officials in state departments of education, and now into the unseen hands of federal government bureaucrats. School administrators must comply with the requirements set by educational specialists who run their state departments of education, and by the bureaucrats who work at the federal Department of Education, *as well as* the various professional organizations that are developing national standards for their special content fields.

Such power and control, however, was never intended to be given to the federal government, according to the Framers of the Constitution. Since the Constitution does not *grant* the power to oversee the education of its citizens to any one branch of the federal government, under the 10th Amendment this power is considered one that is "reserved to the States respectively, or to the people." This is a fact that we should not forget as we develop a kingdom vision for education that is both *cultural* and *covenantal.*

Who Writes the Standards?

The carrot of federal funding has been hard for state and local school districts to resist ever since 1965, when Congress passed the Elementary and Secondary Education Act (ESEA) with the justification that it was essential to President Lyndon Johnson's "war" on poverty. Recognizing that some states would hesitate to allow the nose of the federal camel under their tent, the ESEA specifically prohibited development of a *national curriculum*.[26] Now that Education Secretary Duncan has called for eliminating "the extreme variation in standards across America," such a national curriculum may soon become a reality. Who is going to write it, and what will it look like? Actually, it's almost already in place, and it will take just a little tweaking by state and federal bureaucrats, and professional educators, to make it standard and uniform across the states to the satisfaction of Mr. Duncan.

To find out how this has happened before our very eyes, all

we need to do is recall once again Bill Clinton's Goals 2000. In passing his education reform agenda, Congress enacted three laws: 1) Goals 2000: Educate America Act (referred to as "Goals 2000); 2) the School-to-Work Opportunities Act (STW); and 3) the appropriations bill for these, HR6. Although the first two bills laid out the plan, as Allen Quist explains, HR6 set forth the means for the plan to be carried out, and the saying "the devil is in the details," was never more true than in this instance. Specifically, HR6 in Title X, Section 10601, (1) (A) states:

> The Secretary [of Education] is authorized to carry out a program to enhance the third and sixth National Education Goals[27] by educating students about the history and principles of the United States, including the Bill of Rights, and to foster civic competence and responsibility.[28]

How was the secretary to carry out such a program to educate students? He couldn't—unless he found a way to develop a *national curriculum* that would tell teachers *what* they were to teach on these subjects, as well as *how* they were to teach it, so that students develop the proper attitudes and dispositions that would incline them to carry out their civic responsibilities.

But those who wrote this bill didn't leave the Secretary without additional direction for his task. They also mandated in section (B) that:

> Such programs shall be known as "We the People: The Citizen and the Constitution." (2) The programs shall (A) continue and expand the educational activities of "We the People: The Citizen and the Constitution" program

administered by the Center for Civic Education; and (B) enhance student attainment of challenging content standards in civics and government.[29]

Here's the answer to *who* is going to write the national curriculum. As Allen Quist states, "It's difficult to overstate the significance of this law…. This one organization, the Center for Civic Education (CCE) will determine, by force of federal law, what must be taught in all our nation's schools regarding civics and government."[30] The 1995 edition of the text *We the People*[31] has been used by high schools across the country with the following results, according to the CCE's website:

> Students involved in the *We the People* program develop greater commitment to democratic principles and values, according to a study by Richard Brody of Stanford University. The study concludes that the program is effective in promoting political tolerance because participating students feel more politically effective and perceive fewer limits on their own political freedom.[32]

The result? Students gain greater "political tolerance." Apparently tolerance is now the highest and most desirable civic and moral virtue in our society.

The New Federal Curriculum and World Citizenship

Of course, Secretary Duncan is going to have to draw upon more than just the Center for Civic Education's *National Standards for Civics and Government.*[33] But George W. Bush's No Child Left Behind Act has taken care of that. It requires all the states to adopt standards in mathematics and other areas and, in turn, to base their student achievement tests on these same standards.[34]

Rather than developing their own content standards, states have turned to professional organizations such as the National Council for the Social Studies.[35] The thematic organization of these standards is intended "to provide a framework for social studies curriculum design." This framework is organized into "themes that represent a way of organizing knowledge about the human experience in the world. The learning expectations ... describe democratic dispositions/purposes, knowledge, and intellectual processes that students should exhibit in forms/students products as the result of the social studies curriculum."[36]

There is too little space here to delve into the details of what is troubling about this description. However, a couple of observations can be made: First, the framework presupposes a relativistic view of human knowledge—man is the measure of his own experience and he organizes or "constructs" his own knowledge about it. Second, the "learning expectations" for students to develop certain "dispositions" takes the content of the instruction out of the cognitive realm and puts it into the affective. How do we shape student's feelings, inclinations, and attitudes so they are disposed to act "democratically" in a situation? This is an ethical and moral question—but it is disguised as a matter of intellectual content knowledge. This is "values education" in disguise.

In reviewing the overall content of the new "Federal Curriculum" expressed in various sets of standards, Quist concludes that the seven objectives listed below "are infused throughout the New Federal Curriculum:"

1. Undermining national sovereignty.
2. Redefining natural rights.
3. Minimizing natural law.
4. Promoting environmentalism.

5. Requiring multiculturalism.

6. Restructuring government.

7. Redefining education as job skills.[37]

The curriculum of the 21st century that our government-controlled public schools are feeding children might best be described as "mother earth, animal planet, and the global village." Eco-education and global education dominate children's minds so that they are now suffering anxiety over the planet. One article in all seriousness claims that in view of students' anxieties, "Experts suggest getting them involved in a recycling program or planting a garden."[38] Globalization is the new "conceptual rubric" in all the disciplines, ranging from anthropology to political science, and is certainly impacting education with full force. Although some use the terms "transnationalism" and even "post-nationality," the term "globalization" is being used to identify "forces of change" that result in "deterritorialization of economic, social, and cultural practices from their traditional moorings in the nation state."[39]

Educational programs such as the International Baccalaureate, which promotes "world citizenship," are now attracting parents who are told that IB schools are not "elitist," but that the curriculum focuses on "international perspectives of learning and teaching." In fact, the IB World Schools are yet another means by which students are being indoctrinated into a transnationalist worldview that sees national sovereignty as an obstacle to world peace and understanding.

The number of IB World Schools in the U.S. has doubled in the last four years and now totals 1,007. There are 2,661 IB World Schools in 136 nations around the globe. The U.S. Department of Education has awarded funds to middle schools to participate and become feeder schools for IB high schools. Among their partnerships they count UNESCO, which has recognized them as a NGO of UNESCO since 1970. "IB representatives participate regularly in UNESCO meetings and comment on UNESCO proposals in education," according to the IB website.[40]

Kingdom Citizens Living in the Covenant Village

Even as our nation's leaders seem bent on bringing us into subjection to some form of transnational world government—whether economic or political, or both,[41] the need to provide a *cultural* and *covenantal education* for Christian children could never be greater. But that education cannot be driven by a false ideology of "world citizenship." Our covenant children and youth are not citizens of *this* world. We are citizens of a *heavenly* kingdom, one we have been *transplanted* into by God's grace.[42] It is His kingdom and none other that we are here to promote.

The fact is, as Rodney Stark points out in the concluding chapter of *The Victory of Reason: How Christianity Led to Freedom, Capitalism, and Western Success,* it is not democracy, or capitalism, or even modernity that is spreading around the globe the fastest. It is Christianity.[43] As Philip Jenkins has documented, Christianity is growing in "the south." The southern hemispheres—Latin America and Africa, are indeed experiencing phenomenal growth in Christianity.[44]

Our goal is not transnational or multicultural education, but *intergenerational* education for virtue. Such an education prepares our children to worship the Lord and love Him with all their heart, soul, mind, and strength. It prepares them to live in the sweetness of fellowship and communion with other believers and followers of the Lord Jesus Christ. It shows them how to work heartily "as unto the Lord" and to see their daily lives as moment by moment redemptive acts, bringing the culture into submission to the rule of the Lord Jesus Christ, for His glory and the praise of His name.

Such an education should cultivate in the hearts of learners a desire to share with others the stories of His work in their lives. It should give them the knowledge and skills to serve as citizens of their nations in the formation, transformation, and preservation of cultural institutions built upon godly principles and structures. It should enable them to see God's creative work in His marvelous creation and its spectacular glory and beauty as but a tiny reflection of God's perfections and His all-surpassing glory.

In the introduction to the second edition of her book, *It Takes a Village*, Hillary Clinton says, "'It takes a village' has never had more meaning as a concept than it does today. Beyond assembling the local support team it takes to raise a child well, *we need to come together globally* to create conditions that provide all children everywhere hope and opportunity [emphasis added]."[45] "We need to come together globally," is the current mantra chanted by education and government leaders alike.[46] Yet, there is no "global village" apart from the Body of Christ! In Him we are one and any other "global community" is only a counterfeit.

In raising our children covenantally, as Susan Hunt reminds us in *Heirs of the Covenant: Leaving a Legacy of Faith for the Next Generation*, "God's covenant relationship with us is to be mirrored in our relationships with one another. God tells us this in His Word, and He showed us what it looks like in the person of Jesus. Show and tell is a powerful method of teaching." Hunt continues with the profound truth, "We show and tell what we believe all the time. Sometimes we show and tell biblical truth. Sometimes we tell biblical truth and show untruth. If we think we are saying and showing nothing, that silence and passivity is its own message."[47]

As parents, teachers, friends of those with children, as friends of children, as relatives of children, or whatever our relationships, we are all living together, teaching, and learning from one another in a "covenant village." In Susan Hunt's words:

In the covenant village, there is a sense in which all of the villagers are teachers and all are students all the time. Of course the teacher/student relationship is closer and more intentional in formal teaching situations, but the principles ... apply to all. They apply in the home and in the church as we show and tell what we believe.[48]

In the following chapter we will describe in more detail what this "covenant village" might look like if we were all captured by the same kingdom vision of education for our children—one that is both *covenantal* and *cultural*.

Chapter Ten

COVENANTAL AND CULTURAL EDUCATION

I t takes a *covenant village* to equip young people to enter life as agents of Christian influence, but there's a problem. Too few of us sign up to be active members of the *covenant community*. That's because, as Susan Hunt points out, covenant community "is so foreign to our fallen natures that our redeemed natures struggle to believe and practice it. The cultural bent to privatization and individualism is nothing new."

Soon after the fall, Cain's defensive response, "Am I my brother's keeper?" set the pattern for mankind's rebellious refusal both to live in covenantal relationship with God and to reflect that relationship by loving others as He loves us.[1]

Urban planners are now trying to build "sustainable communities" where people can live and shop and participate in community life. They recognize that not only are communities breaking down, but there is a "breakdown in civil society." "Every year over the last decade or two," says one commentator, "millions have withdrawn from the affairs of their communities."[2]

Another says, "American suburban communities do seem to be chilly places. Devoid of people during the day, they are filled with people sitting behind television or computer screens in the evenings...."[3] People are so preoccupied with their own affairs it seems they have neither the time nor the inclination to become involved in civic affairs.

Churches are suffering from the same malaise. Many local congregations struggle to maintain healthy attendance. There seems to be a general disinterest and disinclination to participate in church activities. Research shows that 23 percent of Americans are "unattached" from either a "conventional church" or "an organic faith community." Yet within this group, six out of ten adults (59 percent) consider themselves to be Christian, one-fifth (19 percent) read the Bible, and three out of every five (62 percent) pray to God during a typical week.[4]

If the church is going to recover from its own malaise before more signs of ill health appear, we must recognize that these attitudes are symptomatic of the infection gripping the broader culture. Then we must acknowledge how the culture is influencing us—even within the church.

Distinguishing Ourselves From the Culture

If education is to be both *covenantal* and *cultural*, it must first be distinguishable from the surrounding culture. This is no easy task! It has been a problem for the individual Christian, as well as for the church as a whole, ever since Christ left his disciples on the Mount of Olives gazing up into heaven in rapt awe. We may be "in the world, but not of it," but sometimes this leaves us feeling out of place and uncomfortable in our uniqueness.

"We like to run in packs. We like to have a buddy. We want to feel accepted by a group," notes Susan Hunt.[5] However, that is a problem when the "pack" we run with is the world and its ways—and when secular culture takes the place of the covenant community in the life of our children and youth. Our responsibility in *covenantal education* is to provide Christian community and church life that is a true demonstration and acknowledgement of the "grace wherein we stand." It is a community that lives together in fellowship and awareness that we are all living "before the face of God" in all that we do and in all of our cultural endeavors.

The challenge we face in trying to live this out in the context of a rotting culture is colossal. Throughout history, many Christians have tried to resolve the dilemma of being "in the world, but not of it" by assuming a negative attitude and defensive posture toward their surrounding culture. We face that temptation when enticed to build and live in a *parallel* Christian culture, where we are supposedly safe from the influences of the world. But we are not to be *anti-cultural,* and before we conclude that our present culture is more ungodly than any previous one, we should take a deep breath and consider this reminder from Henry R. Van Til about what the first century church faced.

> The *world*, against which the New Testament warned the primitive church, was forever impinging on the Christian's consciousness. The Christian could not close his eyes and mind to the Graeco-Roman culture of his day, with its amphitheatre and arena, its Pantheon and Parthenon, its forum and temples, its Stoicism and Epicureanism....[6]

It should be clear that our job as parents and teachers in carrying out the task of *covenantal-cultural education* is no less challenging than it was for the fathers and mothers whom Moses addressed in his farewell in Deuteronomy 6. It is the same task David spoke of in Psalm 78—"Telling to the generation to come the praises of the LORD, And His strength and His wonderful works that He has done" (Psalm 78:4).

Living in Cultural Hubs—Keeping a Covenantal Perspective

It is our job as parents, teachers, and fellow church members to make our families, churches, and all of our associations *cultural hubs* where our children can find a nurturing community of covenantal fellowship. We cannot isolate our children from the culture, but must prepare them to go out and be salt and bring light. This includes conveying a mindset that assumes that God's ways are "normal" and the world's are "strange"—and not the other way around![7]

In these hubs our children can find relationships with both their elders and their juniors. They can learn from their mature elders, who have wisdom gained from walking with the Lord through valleys and over mountaintops, and they can share with those who are both younger chronologically as well as younger in the faith. They can participate in the joys of celebration and the sorrows of loss. They can look to heroes of faith and follow models of grace and be mentored by those who have hope for the future and love for their generation. We should treasure our children and youth by raising them in a community and in a culture that is filled with the vitality of faith that comes from living with a *covenantal perspective* before the Lord.

I appreciate the way Susan Hunt describes this covenantal perspective:

> Scripture clearly teaches that the content of God's covenant is to be contextualized in the covenant community. If the covenant is taught in a purely academic way, it will be anemic. God never intended the passing on of the covenant to be just a mental exercise. The covenant is corporate. Our relationship with God is personal and individual, but when that relationship is established, we are immediately in community with others who are in relationships with Him. His grace-relationship with us is the *power* that transfers us from the City of Destruction into the Community of Faith and the *pattern* for how we are to relate to others in this community.

> There is a correlation between the *content* of the covenant and the *context* of the covenant relationship of God's people with one another. The

content of the covenant is to be pushed out into all of life.[8]

Many, such as Susan Hunt, have written about the task of Christian education with great insight and passion. I've been able to draw from these sources in writing this book. Thus, I don't claim to be adding anything new to our understanding of what we should be doing to teach and train the next generation in the content of the covenant. But I am writing out of a grave concern that although we know *what* we should be imparting to the next generation, and we have some good ideas of *how* we should do it, we are not carrying it out as a community of faith with the consistency and the commitment necessary to save the coming generations from the cultural onslaught rising against them. The church as a whole has not made this a priority, and local churches have, in far too many cases, acted as if the nurture and training of their youngest members were solely the responsibility of parents.[9]

Biblically speaking, the responsibility for developing godly character and imparting a biblical worldview does rest "squarely on the shoulders of the parents." As Roy Zuck says, "The Bible views fathers and mothers as teachers—those who instruct their own in the ways of God."[10] Zuck also points to the multigenerational influence of grandfathers and grandmothers and even great-grandfathers before them. However, even this multigenerational responsibility within families does not negate the important biblical truth that the entire Christian community bears responsibility as well.

Covenantal thinking, which should pervade every aspect of the life of the church, says that every child born into the home of Christian parents is extremely precious in God's eyes. Each child placed by God into the home of Christian parents by His sovereign plan has the opportunity to grow and learn through the nurture and admonition of those who love God and seek to follow His commands. If that child's parents are members of a faith community—a local church committed to living as a covenant community in the way Susan Hunt has described—the child will also grow up among those who are pushing the content of that covenant out into all areas of life. Worshipping together, fellowshipping together, challenging each other in love, as all endeavor to grow as disciples and followers of the Lord Jesus Christ with the earnest desire to see His will done "here on earth as it is in heaven."

Human Cultural Endeavor—Tending the Garden

So how do we describe the *cultural* aspect of this vision of education? Is it *counter*-cultural or *anti*-cultural, or even an idealized view that somehow the church should be isolated and develop its own *Christian* culture? If anything, it is a vision that can be described as Tullian Tchividjian does, as "a counterculture for the common good—to live against the world for the world."[11] Such a culture provides a *qualitatively different medium* for nourishing our children's growth and giving them the proper nutrients to develop a biblical worldview and understanding of the world around them.

As noted already, such a cultural milieu may, in fact, make the ways of the world seem "strange," if the cultural medium our children are feeding on is saturated with a *coram Deo—soli Deo gloria* attitude in the daily effort to push the content of the covenant into all of life. When "the world's ways seem normal and God's ways seem strange,"[12] we have lost any hope of educating our children "to live against the world for the world."

All our efforts to provide a *cultural medium* for the growth of our children must be grounded in a biblical understanding of the importance of "human effort and labor expended upon the cosmos, to unearth its treasures and its riches and bring them into the service of man for the enrichment of human existence unto the glory of God," which is how Henry Van Til defines the concept of *culture*.[13] "Culture then does not belong exclusively to the so-called *civilized* nations," says Van Til, "but is the activity of man as image-bearer of his Creator in forming nature to his purposes. Man is a cultural creature, and civilization is merely the external side of culture."[14]

What gives all of our effort and labor in cultural pursuits meaning is our faith in God. From the beginning, we were created to be co-laborers with God. When God directed Adam in Genesis 1:28 to be fruitful and multiply, replenish the earth, and have dominion over all, He was not telling Adam to do this on his own without His assistance! For the Christian who sees Christ as the "cosmic Redeemer, the one through whom all things are restored to the Father,"[15] there is no room for any kind of anti-culturalism in our thinking. Culture is human enterprise—it is not eco-systems or prairie dog colonies. Furthermore, since it is a human social enterprise, as Van Til points out:

> The family is the simplest and smallest unit of society and the real fountain of culture. If this fountain remains pure, man's culture has promise; but if it becomes polluted, all the rest will turn to dust and ashes, since the home is the foundation of the entire social structure.[16]

Thus it comes back again to the necessity of parents modeling interest and involvement in Christian cultural activities in the home in order to set the pattern for their children. This should start, as Dr. D. James Kennedy and Dr. Jerry Newcombe wrote in *Lord of All*, with children seeing that:

> their parents are truly concerned with the things

that are talked about on Sunday, that they have a passion for lost men and women, that they have a desire to share the gospel and to live a godly life, that they are honest, and that their conversations reveal an integrity that is consonant with the Christian faith they profess.[17]

This is the foundation of a culture that is God-glorifying—one that pushes the content of the covenant into all of life.

Worldview vs. Worldliness

Earlier in this chapter I spoke about the need to provide our children and youth with the *mental equipment* to aid them in taking the preserving salt and revealing light of God's truth into the surrounding culture. Sadly, it seems that rather than taking God's truth *out* into the culture, the church has brought untruth from the culture *inside* the church. Evidence of this is the lack of biblical thinking so often found among church members. George Barna reports in *Think Like Jesus*:

> Among all born-again adults, about one-quarter make their moral and ethical choices on the basis of the Bible. One out of five base their choices on whatever feels right. One out of twelve rely on what parents taught in terms of values and principles. Another one out of ten born again adults do whatever will minimize conflict, while lesser proportions of the group trust various other approaches. In essence, *this tells us that three out of four born-again Christians overlook the Bible as their shaping worldview influence.* . . . If we accept the idea that the Bible conveys God's timeless and

unchanging truths, then the survey results are
nothing less than shocking. [Emphasis added.][18]

Where are our children and youth going to get the necessary
armaments to repel the aggressive ideological and moral attacks
that come against them on all sides? Where are they going to
go if their "supply depots"—the cultural hubs of their families,
churches, and other Christian associations—are poorly stocked
and lack the basic understanding and knowledge of biblical
truth that is both our offensive and defensive weapon against the
world's lies?

In his book, *Transforming Children Into Spiritual Champions,*—
which I recommend as essential reading for every parent, pastor,
and teacher—George Barna points out that by age 13, a child's
basic worldview is set. Barna says, "My tracking of religious beliefs
and behavior for more than a quarter century has revealed that the
spiritual condition of adolescents and teenagers changes very little,
if at all, as they age. When significant change is evident, it usually
is attributable to a dramatic intrusion of the Holy Spirit into their
lives."[19] Barna makes the strong claim that "the great myth of
modern ministry" is that "adults are where the Kingdom action
is"—given that the age when the human character and mind is
most malleable and subject to influence is between ages 5-12:[20]

> If you want to shape a person's life—whether
> you are most concerned about his or her moral,
> spiritual, physical, intellectual, emotional or
> economic development—it is during these crucial
> eight years that lifelong habits, values, beliefs and
> attitudes are formed.[21]

Hopefully, Barna's book will rekindle the vision Charles

Spurgeon expressed in his little book *Spiritual Parenting*:

> The best of the church are none too good for this work. Do not think because you have other service to do that you should take no interest in this form of holy work, but kindly, according to your opportunities, stand ready to help the little ones, and to cheer those whose chief calling is to attend to them. To all of us this message comes: "*Feed My Lambs.*" To the minister and to all who have any knowledge of the things of God the commission is given. See to it that you look after the children that are in Christ Jesus. Peter was a leader among the believers, yet he fed the lambs.[22]

It is no stretch to claim that "spiritual parenting" includes "worldview parenting." However, as long as Christians are living lives that are compromised by acceptance of unbiblical worldviews, we are no different from the ostrich God speaks of in Job 39. "She forgets that a foot may crush them, Or that a wild beast may break them. She treats her young harshly, as though they were not hers." It will be very hard to equip children with a biblical worldview unless their parents and adult role models in the covenant community are fully equipped too!

In his book, *Habits of the Mind*, James W. Sire characterizes an *intellectual* as "one who loves ideas." Someone who "loves ideas," he writes, might engage with them by "turning them over and over," "stacking them atop one another," "playing with them," "laughing at them," etc., even "inviting them to dine and have a ball, but also suiting them for service in a workaday life."[23]

We don't have to be Christian *intellectuals*, nor do we have to be able to name every logical fallacy that comes our way to be able to handle ideas and "suit them for service in a workaday life," as Sire advocates. If we are not equipping our children and youth to consider ideas critically and view them through a grid of biblical truth, then all the other mental equipment that we may give them is wasted. When they enter the arena of cultural combat, they will be no match against the lions and gladiators who seek their blood.

As Christians, we should be able to approve those things that are excellent (Romans 2:18; Philippians 1:10) because we know the truth so well that we can recognize the counterfeit. The ways of the world should stand out before us as strange and even grotesque. To survive the cultural war being waged against them, our children and youth need to be fitted with spiritual and intellectual antennae. They must be able to detect the preposterous and perverted as well as the subtle and sanguine untruths that continually assault them through the media, pop culture and in government controlled schooling. They need the pure and powerful armature of the truth to protect them spiritually, mentally, and emotionally from such assaults. Doing anything less is not feeding His lambs. It is sending them to the slaughter.

Covenantal-Cultural Education Requires Kingdom Vision

There *is a global conflict* raging, and it is not just between Western Civilization and Islam, or between terrorism and democracy, or between liberal-progressivism and conservatism. It is a fight between Christ and Satan—between those who are redeemed in Christ and members of His kingdom and those who serve the god of this world and seek his power. The battlefields are not just in the world in general, but even within the church, within families, and most certainly within our nation's schools. In a powerful lecture, "The Christian View of Education," Cornelius Van Til challenged his listeners bluntly:

> And if you still think that you are involved, really
> involved in the struggle between God and Satan for
> the soul of man in the church and in the home, but
> you are not engaged in it in the school, then you are
> deceiving yourself. You are not engaged in it to the
> fullest extent that you must be engaged in it in the
> home and in the church unless you are engaged in
> it in the fields of culture. [24]

The struggle for our children's souls is real, and that is why we must recognize where it is taking place in the areas of popular entertainment, the media, in higher education, and in elementary and secondary schooling in our nation. We cannot think we will win the struggle for the hearts, minds, and souls of the next generation if we are allowing ourselves to be outflanked by ignoring our schools. If we are concentrating all our resources on our children's spiritual training inside the church, and if parents are modeling kingdom discipleship and building strong relationships with their sons and daughters, and yet they are sending them to government-controlled public schools, we have already been outflanked by the forces of the enemy.

In the final chapter we will look at what is at stake if we do not break the ever tightening grip of government control on families and children in our nation. Let us not be deceived into thinking that their plans are benign and harmless. As we have seen in previous chapters, the government and the educational establishment have a clear agenda to take control of the training of our children *to make them serve the state and its purposes.* Therefore, it is imperative that we make the greatest use of the freedoms that are still ours in order to teach and train our children and equip them with a kingdom vision.

Every local church and denomination in this country should be thinking strategically about how they can make it their highest priority to support Christian schools and Christian education for their children and youth and to assist the parents of their churches who are not able to afford such education on their own. Although denominations in the Reformed and Lutheran tradition have a history of supporting Christian schools, it is becoming evident to the leaders of other denominations, such as the Southern Baptist Convention, that we are at a critical juncture in our nation. The need to provide Christian children with a Christian education has now become critically urgent.

Dr. Morris H. Chapman, president and chief executive officer of the Southern Baptist Convention's Executive Committee, has stated:

> In far too many public schools throughout the country our children are being bombarded with secular reasoning, situational ethics and moral erosion.... If we don't do it [expand Christian education] now, do we risk forever losing the opportunity to build schools for God's glory and the future of our children, grandchildren and the land we love?[25]

Many credit the monks with saving Western Civilization by preserving the manuscripts of the classical writers from the hordes of barbarians who were sweeping across Europe.[26] But to do so, they had to stay cloistered in their monasteries. On the other hand, when reformation came to Europe, it was accompanied by reforms of the system of schooling. Instead of reserving education for the elite classes, both Calvin and Luther placed a high priority on educating the young, because every believer in Christ was understood to be a "prophet, priest, and king" and therefore in need of learning the Scriptures. We've already taken note of Calvin's academy in Geneva and have seen as well how this vibrant view of education was brought over to our country's shores by the Puritans.

Without the schools founded by Calvin, Luther, and the other reformers, the Reformation could not have spread across Europe, nor could it have taken root in the culture. An educated clergy and leaders in medicine, law, and the arts and sciences, took the ideas of Calvin and the reformers and planted them in the culture at large. In fact, the case can be made that the reason the Reformation never had the same impact in England as it did on the continent was because of lack of reforms in English education. Reformer Thomas Cranmer put immense effort into reforming the liturgy of the Church of England, writing two beautifully worded editions of *The Book of Common Prayer*. But in spite of John Calvin's strong urging in letters to him and the young Protestant King Edward VI, Cranmer did nothing to establish a seminary or institute reforms of the colleges before his untimely death as a martyr for the Reformation in 1556.[27]

Therefore, for the broader culture to be impacted and even transformed, the church at large in America must ensure that its children are receiving a thoroughly Christian education—one that will develop in them a biblical worldview and one which will enlarge their vision for both the kingdom of Christ and their place in it. Without this, we will never achieve the true revival in our nation for which so many are praying. Without this, we will only continue to bring people in the front door through evangelism and lose them out the back door when they become "unattached" from the church during their 20s and 30s.

As Cornelius Van Til has written in *Essays on Christian Education:*

> Through preaching and teaching in the church and in the home, through the witness borne [by] individual men everywhere, the allegiance of men is

turned away from Satan to Christ. But the warfare is also carried on where you might least expect it. It is carried on in the field of reading and writing and arithmetic, in the field of nature study and history. At every point Satan seeks boys and girls, as well as men and women to take the attitude that he got Eve and Adam to take at the beginning of history. . . .

And now the reason why we are willing as Christian believers in general, and as Christian parents in particular, to sacrifice so largely for the sake of having Christian schools is that we want our children with us to see the vision of the all-conquering Christ as he wrests the culture of mankind away from Satan and brings it to its consummation when the new heavens and the new earth on which righteousness dwell, at last appears.[28]

Chapter Eleven

CONQUERING THE CULTURE FOR CHRIST

O ur children are under attack. The attack is two-pronged—through the media and popular culture *and* through government-controlled schools. On the one hand, popular culture and entertainment media are filling children's minds with images and icons that are sexualized, even pornographic. The same media sidelines or shuns God and Christian morality at every turn.

On the other hand, schools are using curriculum standards that must conform to federal regulations and promote the United Nations' goals, not the historic ideals of our republic. Higher education has become a place for intellectual repression, not inquiry. Students are indoctrinated at every level to love the earth, view humans as a blot on the planet, show tolerance for sin, and strive to be global citizens. The values of traditional morality, Christianity, and republican constitutional government are scarcely seen.

In contrast to this picture of a culture that is growing darker and more inhospitable to Christians, I have tried to draw a picture of hope. That picture is based on God's truth—the truth that our covenantal children and youth, the coming generation, are among the greatest treasures God has given to the church.

Our children are not only our hope for the future, they *are* the future—the future of the church and the future of this culture. They are like arrows, as Psalm 127 says, that we shoot forth to carry our dreams for the future, our hope for the coming of the kingdom, and our hope for the redemption of this culture through Christ. In reference to this Psalm, Dennis Rainey points out in *A Call to Family Reformation,* "God designed children to be crafted, aimed, and released for battle—spiritual battle."[1] God will use these arrows, if He so chooses, to scatter His enemies as David sings of in his "Song of Deliverance" in 2 Samuel 22. If God graces our nation with revival, it may well come through our children—

not through us.

Therefore, it is our responsibility, as the "elder generations" in the church, to diligently protect the liberty we have to educate and nurture our children according to God's commands. This should be our first priority, above personal goals and ambitions, or pleasures, above involvement in our local churches, and above civic involvement. For what can compare to gaining all these and losing the most precious gift God has given us—our children?

New Threats to Christian Education

To stem the negative cultural tide coming through media and popular culture, we must use every communication platform possible to proclaim a vision of hope and redemption. We also must ensure that cultural space stays open where we can form Christian associations and organizations. These serve a vital function as spiritual *hubs* where we can gather and practice discipleship and enjoy fellowship. Like the spokes that radiate from the hub of a wheel, such associations provide avenues to reach out into the culture. Whether it's our local church, a Christian ministry, the local Christian school, a music group, or a Christian chamber of commerce, each of these organizations not only strengthens those who participate in them, they serve as Christian conduits into the community—assuming, of course, that we also *invite others* to join us in our activities!

We must protect our freedom to form Christian social units and structures. It is a precious liberty that many of our brothers and sisters around the world never experience, and there are those who would take it from us. If secularists had their way, one of the Christian institutions they would shut down is private Christian education. In the book, *The Bible and the Blackboard,* Sam Kastensmidt points out how state authorities try to "bully" private Christian schools.

One example is the case of Calvary Chapel Christian School (CCCS) in Murrieta, California. At the time Kastensmidt wrote in

2007, CCCS and the Association of Christian Schools International had brought a suit against the University of California. They alleged that UC had discriminated against them because the university refused to accept credits from the Christian high school. The university argued that the CCCS curricula did not "offer a nonbiased approach."[2]

On August 8, 2008, U.S. District Judge S. James Otero announced his decision, ruling against Calvary Chapel Christian School and the Association of Christian Schools International.[3] That same day, CCCS appealed to the Ninth Circuit Federal Court of Appeals. The following excerpts from the school's website describe their case:

> This unprecedented lawsuit centers on whether the UC school system can discriminate against private religious schools by denying recognition of college preparatory courses taught by religious high schools, merely because the courses are taught from a religious perspective.... The lawsuit contends that the UC school system has recently refused to approve over 150 courses that were intended to be taught by Christian, Catholic, and Jewish high schools merely because they were to be taught from a religious viewpoint. The lawsuit argues that the UC has a practice of requiring private religious schools to teach from a secular perspective if they want recognition of their college preparatory courses. Calvary Chapel and ACSI argue that the UC is attempting to force Christian schools to water down their teaching.... This case is about the future of private religious education....

> The appeal to the Ninth Circuit will argue that the District Judge applied the wrong legal principles as articulated by the U.S. Supreme Court and disregarded mountains of evidence showing the UC's practice of rejecting courses merely because the officials disagree with the religious perspective from which a course may be taught.[4]

The Ninth Circuit Court of Appeals, which will hear the appeal, is the same court that ruled in 2002 that it is unconstitutional to recite the Pledge of Allegiance in public schools because of the words "under God" in the Pledge.[5] Whatever the court decides in this case will have tremendous ramifications for Christian secondary schools across our country.[6]

If the ruling against the Calvary Chapel Christian School is not overturned by the Court of Appeals or, potentially, the Supreme Court, will Christian schools then accommodate to this ruling by compromising content? Will they water down or change courses to "pass muster" with secular state universities and colleges? Or will parents and students pressure their schools to do so, just so all their courses will be accepted at secular schools?

Of course there is another option—students could attend Christian colleges. But, except for a few, Christian colleges are smaller, more expensive, and lacking in prestige. However, they give students the opportunity to learn from professors who can freely teach within a Christian framework and worldview. Sadly though, only a small proportion of Christian high school graduates attend these schools. The majority go off to secular universities within their state—many of them having accepted state scholarships. What opportunities are these young men and women missing because they are opting to take a scholarship to a secular school, rather than sacrifice to attend a Christian college? Can they make the same impact on the culture as those who attended Calvin's Academy in Geneva?

Gary DeMar has accurately noted, "The no-public-education view isn't popular with the majority of Christians. Blasting public education in America is for some akin to blaspheming on holy ground." DeMar identifies a number of reasons given to justify continued support of government-controlled schools, including, "We can't afford it," "My child's a witness in the public school," "I want my child to experience the 'real world,'" and "My kid's school is fine." He answers these and others quite cogently in his book, *Whoever Controls the Schools Rules the World.*[7]

It could be argued, that just as in India, where the Hindu reverence for cows allows them to wander without restraint, public education is just as much a "sacred cow" in America. Here, public education is destroying our "crops"—our children—stopping the traffic of ideas from reaching them, and leaving ugly deposits in our children's minds! Just like the Hindus of India who refuse to slaughter their holy cows while their children starve, too many Christians in America still cling to the holy cow of public education. Meanwhile, their children's minds and hearts are starving for a Christian understanding of the world and culture around them.

One of the largest denominations in our nation is now facing, for the first time, declining numbers. Yet as a denomination, they have never supported Christian education of their young. The conclusion is unavoidable. If our coming generations are not captured by a full-orbed understanding of Christ's call to personal discipleship and the task of transforming the culture under His kingship, then we will continue to see these youths become *disconnected* from their parents and grandparents and *unattached* to the church.

George Barna puts the number of "Casual Christians" in American society at 66 percent of the adult population. The number of "Captive Christians"—those whose lives are defined by their faith—is 16 percent.[8] If those who are *captive to Christ* are not passing that passion on to their children, their numbers will continue to dwindle.

Parental Rights versus Government Control

The threat to Christian education is yet another example of the way secularists, driven by a liberal-progressive ideology that was shaped and radicalized in the '60s, seek complete control over our children's lives. In addition to threats against Christian education, there are a number of other threats on the horizon that have an unprecedented potential to impact all parents' rights to direct their children's upbringing. Each of these threats could wreck havoc to the integrity of the family and therefore they are threats against the foundation of society itself.

Compulsory LGBT Curriculum

On May 26, 2009, by a 3 to 2 vote, the Board of Trustees of the Alameda Unified School District of California approved LGBT (lesbian, gay, bisexual, transgender) lessons as part of a "Safe Schools" anti-bullying curriculum.[9] Second graders will have to read the book, *And Tango Makes Three,* about allegedly homosexual penguins trying to create a family. Fifth graders will study "sexual orientation stereotypes."[10] The author of these lessons is a 5th grade teacher who wrote them after she was contacted by a "homophobic" parent who complained about her "coming out" as a lesbian to her fifth grade class.[11]

Not only does the curriculum *not* address "bullying" as such, other than to include it as a vocabulary word,[12] it does not deal with harassment of students based on race or religion. Although the term "heterosexual" is introduced in 5th grade along with a mandatory parental opt-out notification, the term "homosexual" is introduced in 4th grade, and no parental opt-out notification is provided. Children study the pioneer Donner family—notorious for their cannibalism when stranded on their journey to California in the 1800s—as an example of a "heterosexual family."[13]

The curriculum is compulsory. It does not include an opt-out provision for parents, even though parents may opt-out of the school district's health and sex education classes.[14] The majority of parents who spoke at the board meetings held to discuss the "anti-bullying" curriculum opposed it. Ironically, they were repeatedly booed and hissed when they stood to voice their opposition. But parent opposition did not stop three of the five board members from voting to impose the LGBT indoctrination on students.[15]

With the Alameda and the Calvary Chapel Christian School cases, we should be praying for the Christian families in California who are facing these attacks! We should also be on the alert for similar programs across the country. As the lead attorney for CCCS and ACSI has said, "Many trends tend to start in California."[16]

Universal Pre-School

Consistent with Secretary of Education Arne Duncan's proclamation that, "We are all part of one system of learning that begins at birth and never stops,"[17] the drive is on to get federally funded and controlled universal pre-school for three and four-year-olds. The American Recovery and Reinvestment Act of 2009, otherwise known as the "stimulus bill," included $5 billion in funding for early childhood education. President Obama is also pushing for an "Early Learning Challenge Grant" program that would give states funds "to implement universal preschool for all three and four-year-old children in the country, regardless of family income."[18]

The claims for these programs are lofty. Proponents of universal Pre-K say they will bring economic benefits to the country and prolonged academic and social benefits to the children. Research done by The Heritage Foundation, the Lexington Institute, the Reason Foundation, and the Public Interest Institute (among others), shows otherwise.[19]

Facts are not likely to deter those determined to promote preschool education using "curricula aligned with early learning standards." The stakes are enormous, however. As the authors of the Lexington Institute article, *Federalizing Pre-K Could Do More Harm than Good*, point out, "Any push by federal and state officials for preschool uniformity could have major implications for the well-being of children, the choices available to families, and even the nature of parenting."[20]

Mandatory Service for Children and Youth?

In his recent book, *Fighting for America's Soul*, Robert Knight noted the expansion of AmeriCorps under a bill signed on April 21, 2009. In May, Gerald Walpin, the Inspector General for AmeriCorps and other national service programs, started investigating AmeriCorps for mishandling funds. In June, as Walpin's investigation was getting underway, President Obama fired him, stating in a letter to the House Speaker and the Vice President, who serves as the President of the Senate, "It is vital that I have the fullest confidence in the appointees serving as Inspectors General. That is no longer the case with regard to this Inspector General."[21]

Aside from the fact that AmeriCorps is now going to get $5 billion over the next five years and $10 billion over the next ten for programs that the Inspector General thought were mishandling funds, there is another aspect to AmeriCorps that we need to watch closely. In the original bill, as Knight points out, there was a provision to create a commission to study "mandatory civilian service." Thankfully, this provision was pulled from the AmeriCorps bill before signing because of "public outcry."[22] However, Washington Rep. Jim McDermott

(D-WA) has reintroduced it as the Congressional Commission on Civic Service Act (H.R. 1444).[23]

The bill, if passed, would set up a commission consisting of leaders in the fields of public service, business and academics. Their task would be to study topics mandated by Congress and report back with their recommendations. The bill lists 12 topics, four of which are radioactive! Except for the bold type for emphasis, I've listed these four just as they are found in the bill.

> *Item 6:* Whether a workable, fair, and reasonable **mandatory service requirement for all able young people could be developed, and how such a requirement could be implemented** in a manner that would strengthen the social fabric of the Nation and overcome civic challenges by bringing together people from diverse economic, ethnic, and educational backgrounds.

> *Item 7:* The need for **a public service academy,** a 4-year institution that offers a federally funded undergraduate education **with a focus on training future public sector leaders.**

> *Item 8:* The means to **develop awareness of national service and volunteer opportunities at a young age** by creating, expanding, and promoting service **options for primary and secondary school students** and by raising awareness of existing incentives.

> *Item 9:* The effectiveness of **establishing a training program on college campuses to recruit and educate college students for**

national service.[24]

Robert Knight provides a good description in his book of what such recommendations could bring. The very idea that the House of Representatives is willing to give serious attention to these is beyond belief! But government-run national service has now become First Lady Michelle Obama's pet project, so no doubt a high powered push from the White House will keep this bill moving.[25]

If mandatory service is made a condition of high school graduation, and if it becomes linked to eligibility for student loans, the government is on its way to having total control over who can attend universities and colleges and who can't. No doubt they would be looking for those who would exhibit the virtue of "tolerance" and have the correct "democratic disposition." Such discrimination is already taking place at some universities.[26]

The Obama administration has already proposed eliminating the Federal Family Education Loan Program, the "public-private sector partnership" which is the primary provider of college loans in America. They claim that this would "save $94 billion over 10 years by eliminating the private lenders and leaving the loans fully controlled by Washington." But this is just another example of the economic sleight-of-hand now commonplace in our government. (A full explanation of what's at stake with this plan can be found in the article referenced in the endnote.[27])

The Push to Sign the UN Convention on the Rights of the Child

As our federal government is enlarging itself by gaining control of more and more sectors of society, we face threats to our children not imaginable a generation ago. Of all the initiatives on the horizon, the most serious threat to families is the UN Convention on the Rights of the Child (CRC).

Liberal-progressive, such as Hillary Clinton and others, have been pushing for the signing of this treaty for years, but there was no thought of signing it in the previous administration. On June 22, 2009, however, U.S. Ambassador to the UN, Susan Rice, told a group of students that the Obama administration is now discussing "when and how it might be possible to join" other nations in ratifying the CRC. Rice claimed that it is a disgrace that the U.S. would stand with Somalia as one of the few nations still opposing this treaty.[28]

What Rice didn't say is that unlike most other nations, any treaty signed by the United States under the Constitution's Supremacy Clause in Article VI supersedes any state or federal laws contrary to its provisions. In essence, we would be throwing away our national sovereignty in regard to parental rights. Only days before Rice made her speech, the UN ramped up the requirements of the CRC. As ParentalRights.org reported:

> On June 17, 2009, at the UN headquarters in Geneva, the UN's Human Rights Committee— which oversees all human rights treaties— announced that it was forming a committee to draft a new "protocol" for the UN Convention on the Rights of the Child. **Under this new addition to the CRC, individual children would be able to file a formal legal complaint if they believe that their rights had been violated. It would give this new international tribunal the right to determine if the child's treaty rights had been violated by any person.** [Emphasis added.][29]

The very real possibility that this administration would sign the CRC if there's no serious opposition to it has prompted the introduction of a Parental Rights Amendment in Congress. Rep.

Peter Hoekstra (R-MI) has introduced House Joint Resolution 42 in the House of Representatives, and Sen. Jim DeMint (R-SC) has introduced it in the Senate as Senate Joint Resolution 16.[30] As Senator DeMint explained:

> Now we're finding that parental rights are being attacked by courts all over the country, and as we look at where this country is going—particularly [regarding] more association with the United Nations and [consideration of] the U.N. Convention on the Rights of the Child, these treaties would supersede all the laws in 50 states.[31]

Just a few examples of the provisions of the CRC will give you a sense of how this could impact your parenting along with everyone else. Imagine if your 13-year-old disagreed with the curfew you have set for her. This treaty gives her the "right to be heard" by a governmental agency, which could then review your decision to determine if it was in accord with the "best interest of the child" principle of the treaty. Or, how about those chores your 16-year-old son is expected to do to retain the privilege of using the family car? Well, he can tell you that this week he doesn't have time to do them because he needs to get in his necessary amount of leisure time— something that, according to the CRC treaty, is one of his "legally enforceable rights."[32]

There's more—a lot more. Visit www.ParentalRights.org to become fully informed about the danger and about what is being done to protect us from this attack on families. Michael Farris, President of ParentalRights.org, has pointed out the monumental effect The UN Convention on the Rights of the Child CRC treaty could have if it were to be signed by the United States.

Everything relative to a child is in the treaty.... The ability of parents to choose the religious upbringing of their children would be challenged under the treaty. And you give the government the ability to say, we don't really think that your religious point [of view] is in the best interest of the child.[33]

Watchmen on the Walls

Education expert Eric Buehrer called in 1995 for a paradigm shift away from the idea that schools are "*the* remedy for society's problems."[34] Instead, Buehrer recommended that schools focus on giving students a solid academic foundation and quit trying to be one-stop social service agencies.

That did not happen. Instead, the dominant paradigm now is "*government* is the remedy." Wherever there's a problem, *government* must step in to fix it. Individual freedoms, individual liberties, as well as religious freedoms and liberties are all in danger of being swept away in the tsunami of government programs coming our way.

The question is—what can we do?

At the close of his book, *Fighting for America's Soul,* Robert Knight writes:

...if Christians and like-minded citizens did one thing a *month,* it could turn this nation around. It's time to get on our knees and ask God's forgiveness and blessing. Then, we need to roll up our sleeves and get the job done.[35]

In this spirit of prayerful repentance and petitioning for God's help, this chapter has identified some key places where we must continue to be "watchmen on the walls." We must vigilantly protect against judicial activism, government legislation, and anti-Christian political activists that could do great damage to our Christian institutions and families.

This is not the time to despair. Neither is it the time to follow the Australian motto, "She'll be right," which is just a glib and unfounded confidence that things will somehow work out okay. If ever there were a time for concerted action and continued effort in the areas we have been laboring in, now is that time. For decades we've been fighting the culture war against abortion in order to save children in the womb. We've been fighting to protect our children from indoctrination in public schools. We've been fighting to protect traditional marriage between a man and a woman. We've been fighting to keep pornographic programming off the television cable stations and to protect our children from predators on the Internet.

There are some, however, who are calling us to "greater civility" and telling us to "tone down the rhetoric," while smugly claiming that all this effort by Christians in the political arena has brought scant results. "It's time," they say, "for Christians to get back to what their primary focus should be—personal evangelism. All of this 'political action' has only alienated people."

Conquering the Culture for Christ

Such an argument fails on two accounts. First, it fails to recognize or acknowledge that we do not engage in political action for pragmatic reasons. We're not just trying to "change policies," as important as that may be. We are called to bring healing and redemption through Jesus Christ to all spheres of society—including the government. Hence Christians must stay in the political arena— even when it gets bloody. As Dr. D. James Kennedy has pointed out, "Jesus Christ is not only Lord of our souls. He is Lord over politics."[36] Our involvement in the realm of politics and government is a response to God's command in Genesis 1:28 to unfold and bring order to creation. It is also a response to Christ's command in Matthew 28:19-20 to bring His healing and heavenly order to the nations.

Second, we cannot forsake any cultural arena. Wherever the battle rages between the kingdom of Christ and the kingdom of Satan—that is where we must be raising the standard for Christ. Indeed, the battle rages through every social institution and in every part of culture and society, because it rages in the human heart. Yet in the end, as my great-uncle, Cornelius Van Til once wrote:

> He [the believer] knows that his cultural activity will not be in vain in the Lord. . . . He knows that he must fight the battle for a Christian culture first of all within himself and then with those who seek to destroy his faith and with it all true culture. He knows that the weapons of this warfare between a Christian and the non-Christian culture are spiritual.[37]

Great-uncle Kees (using the Dutch spelling of "Case" as my father did) wrote in his *Essays in Christian Education* some words I find highly instructive when I consider the work now before us. As we compare the culture, "which is the expression of darkness for all its seeming brilliance and gaudiness, and that culture which is the expression of the kingdom of light, however insignificant it may seem to be," we cannot "obscure the line of demarcation" between them. Nor should we fail to acknowledge that "to grasp culture without Christ is to lose culture as well as Christ."[38]

Therefore, as I think of the challenge before us—to save our children and youth from the culture "which is the expression of darkness," there are some additional words of encouragement that

I also take from great-uncle Kees.

> "Ye are the salt of the earth," said Jesus to the twelve apostles. By the power of the Holy Spirit, the Spirit of culture par excellence, this little band of uncultured men went out to conquer the world of culture for Christ. By their teaching they saved even non-Christian culture for they made it serve the purposes of the culture of Christ.[39]

Every time I read this paragraph I am filled with emotion. My great-grandfather was such an "uncultured" man. A Dutch tenant dairy farmer, he decided to bring his sons to America rather than let them be conscripted into the Dutch army. One of the traditions he set for his family was reading the Bible with his children after the evening meal. His sons, including my grandfather and my great-uncle Kees, carried on that tradition. So did my father. A heritage of believing was passed from generation to generation.

Now our generation and those after us must do the same. Will we, too, go forth, as did the disciples, in the power of the Holy Spirit to "conquer the world of culture for Christ?" Will we join together as a band of brothers and sisters in Christ, willing to give our utmost for His Highest? Will we build traditions of believing to be passed on from generation to generation? Will we tell our children, as David wrote in Psalm 78, the things "we have heard and known, and our fathers have told us?" Will we inspire them with "His wonderful works that He has done"?

Surely, we can do no less—for the sake of our children—for the sake of the Kingdom—for the sake of our Savior, the incomparable Christ.[40]

ENDNOTES

Foreword

1   C.S. Lewis, *The Abolition of Man* (New York: HarperCollins Publishers, 2001 edition, first published in 1944), 13.
2   Ibid, 5.
3   D. James Kennedy and Norman R. Wise, *Restoring the Truth* (Fort Lauderdale, FL: CRM Publishing, 1987).

Chapter One: What War?

1   "Internet Pornography Statistics," Internet Filter Review, http://www.internetfilter review.com/internet-pornography-statistics.html.
2   Ben Shapiro, "I Got Married Last Week," July 16, 2008. http://benjaminshapiro.com/columns2008.html.
3   Ken Blackwell, "Culture Unraveling," *WORLD Magazine*, April 29, 2009.
4   Ibid.
5   Forum on Child and Family Statistics, *America's Children in Brief: Key National Indicators of Well-Being, 2008* http://www.childstats.gov/americaschildren/eco.asp.
6   National Center for Missing & Exploited Children. *Internet Sex Crimes Against Minors: The Response of Law Enforcement*. Virginia: National Center for Missing & Exploited Children, 2003.
7   K.C. Basile, J. Chen, M.C. Lynberg, L.E. Saltzman. Prevalence and characteristics of sexual violence victimization. Violence and Victims 2007;22(4): 437-448.
8   Ben Shapiro, *Porn Generation: How Social Liberalism Is Corrupting Our Future.* Washington, D.C.: Regnery Publishing, Inc., 2005.
9   CDC. Youth Risk Behavior Surveillance—United States, 2007. *Morbidity & Mortality Weekly Report* 2008;57 (SS-4):1–131.
10 Ray Bohlin, "The Epidemic of Sexually Transmitted Diseases," *Probe Ministries*, 1993, http://www.leaderu.com/orgs/probe/docs/epid-std.html.
11 Associated Press, March 11, 2008. http://www.msnbc.msn.com/id/23574940/
12 B.S. Fisher, F.T. Cullen, M.G.Turner. 2000. The sexual victimization of college women. Washington: Department of Justice (US), National Institute of Justice; Publication No. NCJ 182369.
13 Centers for Disease Control and Prevention (a). Web-based Injury Statistics Query and Reporting System (WISQARS) [Online]. (2005). National Center for Injury Prevention and Control, Centers for Disease Control and Prevention (producer). [2008 April 10] Available from URL: www.cdc.gov/ncipc/wisqars/default.htm.
14 U.S. Department of Justice, Office of Justice Programs, Office of Juvenile Justice and Delinquency Prevention. *Juvenile Justice Bulletin*, April 2009. http://www.ncjrs.gov/

pdffiles1/ojjdp/225344.pdf.

OJJDP publications available at www.ojp.usdoj.gov/ojjdp.

15 ChildStats.gov, Forum on Child and Family Statistics. http://www.childstats.gov/
americaschildren/demo.asp.

16 David Limbaugh, *A Christian Nation?*, Townhall.com, April 10, 2009. http://townhall.
com/columnists/DavidLimbaugh/2009/04/10/a_christian_nation.

17 The Equal Access Act of 1984, 20 U.S.C. §§ 4071-74.

18 Richard Lappert and Robert Simonds, *The Christian World View of Education*,
The Education Committee of the Coalition on Revival, 6. http://65.175.91.69/
Reformation_net/COR_Docs/Christian_Worldview_Education.pdf.

19 R. Albert Mohler, Jr., *Culture Shift: Engaging Current Issues With Timeless Truth*,
Colorado Springs, CO: Multnomah Books, 2008, 17.

20 Bruce Hindmarsh, "Let the Little Children Come to Me," *Christianity Today.
com*, May 27, 2009, http://www.christianitytoday.com/ch/byperiod/earlymodern/
letthelittlechildrencome.html.

21 Ibid.

22 Ibid.

23 Ibid.

24 Lawrence Jones, "Thousands Pray for Spiritual Revival at the Call California,"
ChristianPost.com, November 3, 2008. http://www.christianpost.com/article/2008
1103/thousands-pray-for-spiritual-revival-at-thecall-california/index.html.

Chapter Two: Too Much Schooling, Too Little Education

1   D. James Kennedy and Norman R. Wise, *Restoring the Truth* (Ft. Lauderdale, FL: CRM
Publishing, 1987).

2   Ann Coulter, *Godless: The Church of Liberalism* (New York, NY: Crown Forum, 2006),
151.

3   Robert H. Bork, *Slouching Towards Gomorrah: Modern Liberalism and American
Decline* (New York, NY: Harper Collins Publishers, Ind., 1996), 252.

4   Dartmouth College website: http://www.dartmouth.edu/~reg/courses/desc/colt.
html.

5   Ben Shapiro, *Brainwashed: How Universities Indoctrinate America's Youth* (Nashville,
TN: WND Books., 2004), 2.

6   Martin L. Gross, *Conspiracy of Ignorance* (New York, NY: Harper Collins Publishers,
Inc., 2000).

7   Quoted in David Kupelian, *The Marketing of Evil: How Radicals, Elitists, and Pseudo-
Experts Sell Us Corruption Disguised as Freedom* (Nashville, TN: WND Books, 2005),
152.

8   Thomas Sowell, *Inside American Education: The Decline, the Deception, the Dogmas*
(New York, NY: The Free Press, 1993), 8.

9   The 39th Annual Phi Delta Kappa/Gallup Poll Of the Public's Attitudes Toward The
Public Schools, accessed at: http://www.pdkintl.org/kappan/k_v89/k0709pol.htm.

10 Kupelian, 155.

11 Gary DeMar, *Whoever Controls the Schools Rules the World* (Powder Springs, GA:

American Vision, 2007), 62.

12   Joshua Meyrowitz, University of New Hampshire, quoted by John Leo, "Spicing up the (ho-hum) truth," *U.S. News & World Report,* March 8, 1993, 24.

13   "More American Adults Read Literature According to New NEA Study," January 12, 2009, contact Sally Gifford, giffords@arts.gov, http://arts.endow.gov/news/news09/ReadingonRise.html

14   "Five Out of Seven Core Religious Behaviors Have Increased in the Past Decade According to Barna Survey," Barna Group, April 3, 2006. http://www.barna.org/barna-update/article/5-barna-update/156-five-out-of-seven-core-religious-behaviors-have-increased-in-the-past-decade-according-to-barna-survey

15   Michael Vlach, "Americans and the Bible: Bible Ownership, Reading, Study and Knowledge in the United States," accessed at Theological Studies.org, http://www.theologicalstudies.citymax.com/page/page/1572910.htm.

16   Henry R. Van Til, *The Calvinist Concept of Culture* (Grand Rapids, MI: Baker Book House, 1972), 32.

17   George Barna, *Transforming Children into Spiritual Champions* (Ventura, CA: Regal, a division of Gospel Light, 2003), 34.

18   English Standard Version, Study Bible. Editors: Lane T. Dennis, Wayne Grudem, J.I. Packer, C. John Collins, Thomas R. Schreiner, Justin Taylor (Wheaton, IL: Crossway Bibles, 2008), 341.

19   *Nelson's New Illustrated Bible Dictionary,* General Editor, Ronald F. Youngblood. Nashville, TN: Nelson, 1995, 445.

20   Karen Gushta, *The Concept of "Modeling" in Teacher Education,* unpublished doctoral dissertation, (Bloomington, IN: Indiana University, 2003), 12.

Chapter Three: Worldviews in Disguise

1   Matt Stoller, "Fox News and CNN's Geriatric Audience," March 17, 2007, *MyDD Director Democracy,* http://www.mydd.com/story/2007/3/17/13218/5375.

2   Hitwise Intelligence—Bill Tancer—North America Analyst Weblog. http://weblogs.hitwise.com/bill-tancer/2006/10/of_youtube_web_20_and_early_ad.html.

3   John Gugie, "Smack of Reality #2: Political Commentary Shows Influence Young Voters." Associated Content, Arts and Entertainment, September 16, 2007. http://www.associatedcontent.com/article/381691/smack_of_reality_2_political_comedy.html.

4   Quentin J. Schultze, *Winning Your Kids Back from the Media* (Downers Grove, IL: Intervarsity Press, 1994). Quentin J. Schultze, *Redeeming Television: How TV Changes Christians—How Christians Can Change TV.* (Downers Grove, IL: Intervarsity Press, 1992).

5   Ibid., p. 90.

6   Stephen Colbert, *The Colbert Report,* May 14, 2009, http://www.colbertnation.com/the-colbert-report-videos/227669/may-14-2009/yusuf.

7   Louise Cowan, *The Terrain of Comedy (Studies in Genre),* (The Pegasus Foundation, 1984).

8   Tim McNabb, A Review of Bill Maher's *Religulous,* American Thinker, October 3, 2008.

http://www.americanthinker.com/2008/10/a_review_of_bill_mahers_religu.html.

9 Amanda Carpenter, Hillary's Thesis: "The Village Needs an Enemy," *Human Events. com*, posted 3/09/2007, http://www.humanevents.com/article.php?id=19734.

10 Saul Alinsky, Wikipedia. http://en.wikipedia.org/wiki/Saul_Alinsky.

11 Craig Miyamoto, "Alinsky's Rules for Radicals." http://www.geocities.comWallStreet/8925/alinsky.htm.

12 David Kinnaman and Gabe Lyons, *UnChristian: What a New Generation Really Thinks About Christianity . . . And Why It Matters* (Grand Rapids, MI: Baker Books. 2007), 29-30.

13 Ibid., 31.

14 Quentin J. Schultze, *Winning Your Kids Back from the Media* (Downers Grove, IL: Intervarsity Press, 1994), 17.

15 Carl Kerby, *Remote Control: The Power of Hollywood in Today's Culture* (Green Forest, AR: Master Books, Inc., 2006).

16 Carolyn Moynihan, "Hollywood cleans up teen movie language," *MercatorNet/Family Edge*, posted June 1, 2009. http://www.mercatornet.com/family_edge.

17 David T. Moore, *Five Lies of the Century* (Wheaton, IL: Tyndale House Publishers, Inc., 1995), 245.

18 Robert H. Knight, *Age of Consent: The Rise of Relativism and the Corruption of Popular Culture* (Dallas, TX: Spence Publishing Co., 1998), xxiii.

19 Ibid., 13.

20 Ibid., 99.

21 "A Vanishing Haven: The Decline of the Family Hour," A Special Report of *TV Etc.*, Media Research Center, vol. 7, no. 12, December 1995.

22 "Medial journal raps AMA editor firing," United Press International, February 10, 1999.

23 Knight, 105.

24 John Ankerberg, Craig Branch, and John Weldon, *Thieves of Innocence: Protecting Our Children from New Age Teachings and Occult Practices* (Eugene, OR: Harvest House Publishers, 1993), 27.

25 John Eggerton, "FCC, Justice Dept. ask Supreme Court to overturn appeals court decision throwing out $500,000 fine against CBS," *Broadcasting & Cable*, November 21, 2008. http://www.broadcastingcable.com/article/print/96987-fcc_DOJ_Appeal_Janet_Jackson_To_Supreme_Court.php.

26 James Vicini, "Supreme Court upholds TV profanity crackdown," *Reuters*, April 28, 2009, http://www.reuters.com/article/topNews/idUSTRE53R41K20090428.

27 For example: American Family Association, http://action.afa.net; Media Research Center, http://www.mrc.org/public/default.aspx; Ted Baehr's *Movie Guide http://www.movieguide.org/*.

28 The Federal Communications Commission requires written complaints from viewers for it to take action. You can contact the FCC by writing: FCC, Enforcement Bureau, Investigations and Hearings Division 445, 12th Street SW, Washington, D.C. 20554. You can follow up your written communication by emailing: fccinfo@fcc.gov or calling: 1-888-CALL-FCC (1-888-225-5322) or 1-888-TELL-FCC (1-888-835-5322).

29 Dennis Woods, "Dr. Ted Baehr Interview: His *MovieGuide* Has Broken the Stranglehold of Hollywood Perversity, November 18, 2008, *SearchWarp.com* http: searchwarp.com/swa399342.htm.

30 Ted Baehr's *MovieGuide* can be accessed online at: www.movieguide.org.

31 Ted Baehr and Tom Snyder, "A Hollywood Stimulus Plan: Make More Uplifting Movies," February 13, 2009, *Wall Street Journal,* http://online,wsj.com/article/ SB123449031400180527.html?mod=todays_us_weekend_journal.

32 Ibid.

33 "99 Balloons" http://www.youtube.com/watch?v=th6Njr-qkq0&feature=related.

34 "U.S. regulatory czar nominee wants Net 'Fairness Doctrine,'" April 27, 2009, *WorldNetDaily.com,*
http://www.worldnetdaily.com/index.php?fa=PAGE.view&pageId=96301.

35 Brian E. Fisher, *Media Revolution: A Battle Plan to Defeat Mass Deception in America* (Fort Lauderdale, FL: Coral Ridge Ministries Media, Inc., 2008), 79.

36 D. James Kennedy, *Turn It To Gold,* (Vine Books, 1991). Available from Coral Ridge Ministries at www.coralridge.org or 1-800-988-7884.

Chapter Four: They Banned Prayer and Protected Porn

1 Adrian and Steve Rogers, *Family Survival in an X-Rated World: A Practical Program for Guarding Your Heart and Protecting Your Home* (Nashville, TN: Broadman & Holman Publishers, 2005), 6.

2 Family Safe Media, January 10, 2006, http://www.familysafemedia.com/pornography_ statistics.html.

3 Ben Shapiro, *Porn Generation: How Social Liberalism Is Corrupting Our Future* (Washington, D.C.: Regnery Publishing, Inc., 2005), 136.

4 "Protecting Kids Online." Editorial. *The Washington Post,* July 1, 2004.

5 Accessed at My Kids Browser.com   http://www.mykidsbrowser.com/internetporno-graphy-statistics.php#youth.

6 Ibid.

7 Grant Gross, "Supreme Court refuses Internet age restrictions case," *IT World.com,* January 21, 2009, http://www.itworld.com/legal/61143/supreme-court-refuses-internet-age-restrictions-case.

8 Robert H. Knight, *Fighting for America's Soul: How Sweeping Change Threatens Our Nation and What We Must Do* (Ft. Lauderdale, FL: Coral Ridge Ministries Media, Inc., 2009), 61.

9 Ibid., 62

10 United States Department of Justice, http://www.usdoj.gov/dag/.

11 It is located in the United States Code at 15 U.S.C. § 6501–6506. It was passed as public law as PL 105-277, 112 Stat. 2581-728, enacted October 21, 1998.

12 Children's Online Privacy Protection Act, Wikipedia, http://en.wikipedia.org/wiki/ COPPA.

13 John W. Whitehead, "The Hostile Takeover of Childhood," Commentary, June 15, 2009, *The Rutherford Institute.*

14 Sam Kastensmidt, *Indefensible: 10 Ways the ACLU Is Destroying America* (Fort Lauderdale,

FL: Coral Ridge Ministries Media, Inc., 2006), 13.

15   "ACLU Seeking Explicit Websites on Knoxville School Computers," The American
      Civil Rights Union. http://www.theacru.org/acru/aclu_seeking_explicit_websites_
      on_knoxville_school_computers/.

16   Frank York and Jan LaRue, *Protecting Your Child in an X-Rated World: What You Need
      to Know to Make a Difference* (Wheaton, IL: Tyndale House Publishers, Inc., 2002),
      63.

17   Ibid., 66.

18   ACLU Supports Pornography and Suicide, The American Civil Rights Union, http://
      www.theacru.org/acru/aclu_supports_pornography_and_suicide/.

19   Zachary Gappa, "'Sexting,' Teen Maturity and Parental Responsibility, originally
      posted at *Crosswalk.com*, March 18, 2009. Accessed at Center for a Just Society,
      5/16/2009. http://www.centerforajustsociety.org/press/forum.asp?cjsForumID=1138.

20   Ewen MacAskill, "Obama to Scrap Funding for Abstinence-Only Programmes"
      Guardian, posted 5/08/2009, on the website of the Center for a Just Society, *Word on
      the Street*, http://centerforajustsociety.org.

21   Penny Starr, "Study Critical of Virginity Pledges Reveals That More Religious Teens
      Embrace Abstinence," CNSNews.com, CNS.com Daily E-Brief, 12/31/2008. http://
      www.cnsnews.com/public/content/article.aspx?RsrcID=41356.

22   Phyllis Schlafly, *The Supremacists: The Tyranny of Judges and How to Stop It* (Dallas,
      TX: Spence Publishing Company, 2004), 29-31.

23   William J. Murray, *Let Us Pray: A Plea for Prayer in Our Schools* (New York, NY: William
      Morrow and Company, Inc., 1995), 163.

24   Schlafly, 29.

25   Ibid., 32.

26   Ibid., 57.

27   Ibid., 59-60.

28   Ibid., 60.

29   Ibid., 60-61.

30   Lynn, Barry W., "Civil Rights Ordinances and the Attorney General's Commission:
      New Developments in Pornography Regulation," Harvard C.R.-C.L. L.R. 1986, vol. 21,
      27-125.

31   Archibald D. Hart, *Thrilled to Death: How the Endless Pursuit of Pleasure Is Leaving Us
      Numb* (Nashville, TN: Thomas Nelson, 2007), 3.

32   Saint Augustine, *Confessions*, translated with an Introduction and Notes by Henry
      Chadwick (Oxford: University Press), 3.

33   Shapiro, 6.

34   Joe S. McIlhaney, Jr., MD, and Freda McKissic Bush, MD, *Hooked: New Science on
      How Casual Sex Is Affecting Our Children* (Chicago: Northfield Publishing, 2008),
      Chapter 5.

Chapter Five: Heroes and Heroines: Virtue and Vice Redefined

1   Dave Jackson and Neta Jackson, *The Complete Book of Christian Heroes* (Wheaton, IL:
      Tyndale House, 2004).

2   Adrian Rogers and Steve Rogers, *Family Survival in an X-Rated World: A Practical Program for Guarding Your Heart and Protecting Your Home* (Nashville, TN: Broadman & Holman Publishers, 2005).

3   Madeleine L'Engle, *Herself: Reflections on a Writing Life* (Colorado Springs, CO: WaterBook Press, 2001), 258.

4   "Sounding a warning about an endangered species: Heroes," *Philadelphia Inquirer*, November 25, 1999.

5   Peter H. Gibbon, "Heroes in America" website: http://www.heroesinamerica.org/index.html.

6   Robert H. Knight, *Age of Consent: The Rise of Relativism and the Corruption of Popular Culture* (Dallas, TX: Spence Publishing Co., 1998).

7   Diana West, *The Death of the Grown-Up: How America's Arrested Development Is Bringing Down Civilization* (New York, NY: St. Martin's Griffin, 2007).

8   Knight, 116.

9   Ibid, 122.

10   Gibbon, "Heroes in America."

11   Tom Leonard, "Why I love my private jet, by Oprah Winfrey," my.Telegraph.co.uk, May 12, 2009, http://blogs.telegraph.co.uk/tom_leonard/blog/2009/05/12/why_i_love_my_private_jet_by_oprah_winfrey.

12   David K. Li and Bill Sanderson, "Larry Flynt Buys Purported Nude Photos of Jessica Lynch," Fox News, November 11, 2003, http://www.foxnews.com/story/0,2933,1027 36,00.html.

13   Peter H. Gibbon, "Our Great Ones," *National Review Online*, March 22, 2008, http://www.nationalreview.com/script/printpage.p?ref=/comment/comment-gibbon032203.asp.

14   Coral Ridge Ministries, *Ten Truths About America's Christian Heritage* (Fort Lauderdale, FL: Coral Ridge Ministries Media, Inc., 2008).

15   Michael Scherer, "Obama too is an American Exceptionalist," April 4, 2009, Swampland.blogs. Time.com   http://swampland.blogs.time.com/2009/04/04/obama-too-is-an american-exceptionalist/.

16   Peter H. Gibbon, website, op. cit.

17   Ibid.

18   Ken Gewertz, "Author Calls for Renewal of Honor for Heroes: Admiring Venerable Virtues of Strength, Courage, and Talent," *Harvard University Gazette*, August 22, 2002. http://www.news.harvard.edu/gazette/2002/08.22/11-heroes.html.

19   Quoted by Peter H. Gibbon from the British educator Sir Richard Livingstone, in "Sounding a warning about an endangered species: Heroes," *Philadelphia Inquirer*, November 25, 1999.

20   The results of these three studies, *The Coming Crisis in Citizenship, Failing Our Students, Failing America,* and *Our Fading Heritage,* are included in the Public Interest Institute policy study, *A Republic If You Can Keep It: Failing to Teach First Principles,* Public Interest Institute, April 2009, at www.limitedgovernment.org.

21   Mark Walsh, "Retired Justice's Focus Now on Civic Education Project," April 4, 2008, Education Week online http://www.edweek.org/ew/articles/2008/04/09/32oconnor.h27.

html.Fred Hiatt, "Justice Souter's 'Safe Place,'" *The Washington Post* editorial page, May 25, 2009, http://www.washingtonpost.com/wp-dyn/content/article/2009/05/24/AR2009052401981.html.

22   Knight, *Age of Consent*, 35.

23   Ibid., 39.

24   Colleen Carroll Campbell, "Challenging America's Me-First Culture," *St. Louis Post Dispatch*, May 7, 2009, posted at *Ethics and Public Policy Center*, May 7, 2009. http://www.eppc.org/publications/pubID.3814/pub_detail.asp.

25   Ibid.

26   Ibid.

27   "Narcissist in Chief," *Whistleblower Magazine*, May 2009.

28   Rogers and Rogers, 15.

29   Ibid., 17-27.

30   Gary L. Cass, *Christian Bashing and the Christian Anti-Defamation Commission* (Christian Anti-Defamation Commission, 2007), 119.

31   D. James Kennedy and Jerry Newcombe, *What if Jesus Had Never Been Born? The Positive Impact of Christianity in History* (Nashville, TN: Thomas Nelson Publishers, 1994). See also, D. James Kennedy and Jerry Newcombe, *Lord of All: Developing a Christian World-and-Life View* (Wheaton, IL: Crossway Books, 2005).

Chapter Six: Covenantal Education: Modeling Kingdom Discipleship

1   Diana West, *The Death of the Grown-Up: How America's Arrested Development Is Bringing Down Western Civilization,* (New York, NY: St. Martin's Press, 2007), 71.

2   "Christian Parents Are Not Comfortable With Media But Buy Them for Their Kids Anyway," Barna Research Group, November 19, 2007, http://www.barna.org/.

3   "Young Adults and Liberals Struggle with Morality," Barna Research Group, August 25, 2008, http://www.barna.org/barna-update/article/16-teensnext-gen/25-young-adults-and-liberals-struggle-with-morality

4   West, 70.

5   "The Debt to the Penny and Who Holds It," Treasury Direct® http://www.treasurydirect.gov/NP/BPDLogin?application=np.

6   D. James Kennedy, "Christianity and the Federal Deficit," in *The Mortgaging of America: Biblical Wisdom for a Time of Uncertainty and Change* (Ft. Lauderdale, FL: Coral Ridge Ministries Media, Inc. 2009), 49.

7   A good place to start is: Bat Ye'or, *The Decline of Eastern Christianity Under Islam: From Jihad to Dhimmitude* (Cranberry, NJ: Associated University Presses, 1996).

8   Kristin J. Anderson and Donna Cavallaro, *"Parents or pop culture?: Children's heroes and roles models,"* Find articles at BNET, http://findarticles.com/p/articles/mi_qa3614/is_200204/ai_n9044749/, accessed 6/3/2009.

9   West, 26.

10   Steven Mintz, *Huck's Raft: A History of American Childhood* (Cambridge, MA: Harvard University Press, 2004), 299.

11   West, 92.

12   Rosalind S. Helderman, "Loudoun's New Move: The Tussle." *The Washington Post,*

October 22, 2004. Quoted in Diana West, *The Death of the Grown-Up* (New York, NY: St. Martin's, 2007), 24.

13   "Born again Christians" are defined as people who said they have made a personal commitment to Jesus Christ that is still important in their life today and who also indicated they believe that when they die they will go to Heaven because they had confessed their sins and had accepted Jesus Christ as their Savior. Respondents are <u>not</u> asked to describe themselves as "born again."

14   George Barna, *Growing True Disciples* (Ventura, CA: Issachar Resources, a Division of Barna Research Group, Ltd., 2000), 35.

15   Tullian Tchividjian, *The Kingdom of God: A Primer on the Christian Life* (Glasgow: Hay Nisbet Press, 2005), 13.

16   Ibid., 13-14.

17   John H. Westerhoff, III, *Bringing Up Children in the Christian Faith* (Minneapolis, MN: Winston Press, Inc., 1980), 71.

Chapter Seven: Tolerance: "The Last Virtue"

1   Coral Ridge Ministries *Ten Truths About America's Christian Heritage* (Ft. Lauderdale, FL: Coral Ridge Ministries Media, Inc., 2008).

2   "The True Blue Laws of Connecticut and New Haven," Edited by J. Hammond Trumbull, 1976. http://nhhistory.org/edu/support/nhgrowingup/firstnhteacher.pdf.

3   Sam Kastensmidt, "The Founders and Education," in Gary Cass, Sam Kastensmidt, and Anthony Urti, *The Bible and the Blackboard: Biblical Solutions for Failing Schools* (Ft. Lauderdale, FL: Coral Ridge Ministries Media, Inc., 2007), 25.

4   *The Works of John Adams,* ed. Charles Francis Adams (Boston: Little, Brown & Co., 1854, Vol. VI), 414.

5   Thomas Jefferson, "Letter to John Banister: Advantages of an America Education, 1785," in *Readings in American Educational Thought: From Puritanism to Progressivism,* eds. Andrew J. Milson, Chara Haeussler Bohan, Perry L. Glanzer, and J. Wesley Null (Greenwich, CT, 2004), 69-70.

6   Thomas Lickona, *Educating for Character: How Our Schools Can Teach Respect and Responsibility* (New York, NY: Bantam Books, 1991), 40.

7   Ibid., 7-8.

8   Bruce N. Shortt, *The Harsh Truth About Public Schools* (Vallecito, CA: Chalcedon Foundation, 2004), 298.

9   Ibid., 297.

10   Ibid., 298.

11   Ibid., 297.

12   Gary DeMar, *Whoever Controls the Schools Rules the World,* (Powder Springs, GA: American Vision, 2007), 24.

13   D. James Kennedy and Jerry Newcombe, *Lord of All: Developing a Christian World-and-Life View* (Wheaton, IL: Crossway Books, 2005), 164-165.

14   Cornelius Plantinga, Jr., *Engaging God's World: A Reformed Vision of Faith, Learning, and Living* (Grand Rapids, MI: Wm. B. Eerdmans Publishing Co., 2002), ix.

15   Henry R. Van Til, *The Calvinistic Concept of Culture* (Grand Rapids, MI: Baker Book

House Company, 1972), 115.

16   Ibid.

17   See Cornelius Van Til's essays in Louis Berkhof and Cornelius Van Til, *Foundations of Christian Education: Addresses to Christian Teachers* (Phillipsburg, NJ: Presbyterian and Reformed Publishing Company, 1990).

18   Rousas John Rushdoony, *The Messianic Character of American Education* (Nutley, NJ: The Craig Press, 1963), 19.

19   Ibid., 20.

20   Horace Mann, "Eleventh Annual Report," 1847, p. 218, quoted in Rushdoony, 1963, 22.

21   Steven E. Tozer, Paul C. Violas, Guy Senese, *School and Society: Historical and Contemporary Perspectives* (Boston, MA: McGraw Hill, 1998), 60.

22   Ibid.

23   D. James Kennedy, *Truths That Transform: Great Truths to Touch and Transform Your Life* (Ft. Lauderdale, FL: Coral Ridge Ministries Media, Inc., 1996), 98-99.

24   Rushdoony, 29.

25   Shortt, 306.

26   Ibid., 307.

27   Ibid.

28   John Dewey, "Traditional vs. Progressive Education," an excerpt from *Experience and Education,* 1938, in *Readings in American Educational Thought: From Puritanism to Progressivism,* Eds. Andrew J. Milson, Chara Haeussler Bohan, Perry L. Glanzer, and J. Wesley Null (Greenwich, CT: Information Age Publishing, 2004), 331.

29   *Meno, http://en.wikipedia.org/wiki/Plato%27s_Meno.*

30   In the 1960s, Jerome Bruner revived interest in the work of John Dewey by reintroducing the idea of "learning by discovery." It became popular in a cultural climate where free expression and personal freedom were becoming primary values. The model of A.S. Neill's *Summerhill School,* where students were given freedom to learn what they wanted when they wanted, was tried by some, but curricular adaptations of *discovery learning* that were based on Jerome Bruner's writings found it difficult to survive in the more authoritarian structures required in public school education. However, the idea that all knowledge is *constructed* by the learner, using the information and materials at hand, is dominant throughout American education today—no doubt because it fits so well with the prevailing epistemological and moral relativism.

31   *The Republic of Plato,* translated with notes and an interpretive essay by Allan Bloom (Basic Books, 1968, 1991), 194-195.

32   D. James Kennedy, "To Judge or Not to Judge," Sermon preached at Coral Ridge Presbyterian Church, 2/20/2000.

Chapter Eight: They Closed Down the Marketplace of Ideas

1   "U.S. regulatory czar nominee wants Net 'Fairness Doctrine,'" April 27, 2009, *WorldNetDaily.com,* http://www.worldnetdaily.com/index.php?fa=PAGEview&page Id=96301.

2   Nirmala Punnasami, "No Culture Left Behind?," *CampusReportOnline.net* September

27, 2007, http://www.campusreportonline.net/main/printer_friendly.php?d=1880.

3   Robert A. Bork, *Slouching Towards Gomorrah: Modern Liberalism and American Decline* (New York: NY, Harper Collins Publishers, 1996), 263.

4   Carl Hulse, "Obama Is Sworn In as the 44th President," *The New York Times,* January 20, 2009, http://www.nytimes.com/2009/01/21/us/politics/20web-inaug2.html.
Barack Hussein Obama, Speech at Cairo University, Cairo, Egypt on June 4, 2009, accessed on June 13, 2009 at: http://simerg.com/sidelines/sideline-in-cairo-speech-obama-asks-youth-to-reimagine-and-remake-the-world-progress-must-be-shared/.

5   Bork, 257.

6   Mark Bauerlein, *The Dumbest Generation: How the Digital Age Stupefies Young Americans and Jeopardizes Our Future (Or, Don't Trust Anyone Under 30)* (London: Penguin Books, Ltd., 2008), 13.

7   Brian Fearn, Review of *The Dumbest Generation,* "I am part of the so-called 'dumbest generation' and I liked the book," posted at Amazon.com, September 29, 2008.

8   Josh McDowell, *The Disconnected Generation: Saving Our Youth From Self Destruction* (Nashville, TN: Thomas Nelson, 2000), 8.

9   Ibid., 9.

10   George Barna and Mark Hatch, *Boiling Point: Monitoring Cultural Shifts in the 21st Century,* (Ventura, CA: Regal Books/Gospel Light, 2001), 67.

11   The Barna Group, "New Research Explores How Technology Drives Generation Gap," February 23, 2009, The Barna Group, Ltd., http://barna.org/ http://www.barna.org/barna-update/article/14-media/212-new-research-explores-how-technology-drives-generation-gap.

12   Antidotes to the indoctrination received at secular high schools and universities are available. The following are just several of the ministries that offer a variety of institutes, summer camps, online programs, and seminars for students and adults: Dr. David Noble's **Summit Ministries**, http://www.summit.org/about; Chuck Colson's **Centurions Program**, (see Programs at http://www.breakpoint.org); Dr. Del Tackett and Focus on the Family's **Truth Project** is especially helpful in giving an orientation to the proper roles and responsibilities of the various societal spheres, http://www.thetruthproject.org. **American Vision**, a worldview ministry established in 1978 by Gary DeMar—their vision is, "An America that recognizes the sovereignty of God over all of life, where Christians apply a biblical worldview to every facet of society. This future America will be again a 'city on a hill' drawing all nations to the Lord Jesus Christ and teaching them to subdue the earth for the advancement of His Kingdom," http://www.americanvision.org . Also helpful to university students are the programs of Dr. Frank Turek and **Crossexamined**, (see http://crossexamined.org/). Turek goes to college campuses around the country at the invitation of Christian student groups to give lectures on Christian apologetics and worldview training. **Intervarsity Christian Fellowship** has chapters on 550 U.S. campuses and provides students with seminars and conferences focusing on apologetics, the Christian witness, and missions. The Purpose of InterVarsity Christian Fellowship/ USA is to establish and advance at colleges and universities witnessing communities of students and faculty who follow Jesus as Savior and Lord: growing in love for God, God's Word, God's people of every ethnicity and culture and God's purposes in the

world. http://www.intervarsity.org. Kerby Anderson and **Probe Ministries** offer many resources. Probe's mission is to present the gospel to communities, nationally and internationally, by providing life-long opportunities to integrate faith and learning through balanced, biblically based scholarship, training people to love God by renewing their minds and equipping the church to engage the world for Christ. http://www.probe.org. The Intercollegiate Studies Institute offers summer institutes for students that emphasize the founding principles of "limited government, individual liberty, personal responsibility, the rule of law, market economy, and moral norms" http://www.isi.org/about_isi.html. The Acton Institute also offers programs for students that stress religious liberty and promotion of a "free, virtuous, and humane society." Named after British Lord Acton, a contemporary of Abraham Kuyper and a Roman Catholic, Acton, traced the concept of "liberty of conscience" not back to John Calvin, as did Kuyper, but to Thomas Aquinas.

13   Gary Lyle Railsback, "An Exploratory Study of the Religiosity and Related Outcomes Among College Students," Doctoral dissertation, University of California at Los Angeles, 1994.

14   The Barna Group, "Most Twentysomethings Put Christianity on the Shelf Following Spiritually Active Teen Years," September 11, 2006, The Barna Group, Ltd., http://www.barna.org/barna-update/article/16-teensnext-gen/147-most-twentysomethings-put-christianity-on-the-shelf-following-spiritually-active-teen-years.

15   The Barna Group, "Atheists and Agnostics Take Aim at Christians," June 11, 2007, The Barna Group, Ltd., http://www.barna.org/barna-update/article/12-faithspirituality/102-atheists-and-agnostics-take-aim-at-christians.

16   Allan Bloom, *The Closing of the American Mind: How Higher Education Has Failed Democracy and Impoverished the Souls of Today's Students* (New York, NY: Simon & Schuster, 1987).

17   David Horowitz and Jacob Laksin, *One Party Classroom: How Radical Professors at America's Top Colleges Indoctrinate Students and Undermine Our Democracy,* (New York, NY: Crown Forum, 2009), 6-7.

18   David Horowitz, *Radical Son: A Generational Odyssey* (New York, NY: Simon & Schuster, 1997), 306.

19   Ibid., 415.

20   David Horowitz and Jacob Laksin, 7.

21   Quoted in Gary DeMar, *Whoever Controls the Schools Rules the World* (Powder Springs, GA: American Vision, 2007), 8, from Malachi Martin, *The Keys of This Blood: The Struggle for World Dominion Between Pope John II, Mikhail Gorbachev, and the Capitalist West* (New York: Simon and Schuster, 1990), 251.

22   Horowitz, *Radical Son*, 263.

23   Bork, 113.

24   Bloom, 325.

25   Ibid., 313.

26   Ibid., 326.

27   Ibid., 329.

28 Sol Stern, "Pedagogy of the Oppressor," *City Journal*, Spring 2009, http://www.city-journal.org/2009/19_2_freirian-pedagogy.html.

29 Bill Ayers, Wikipedia, http://en.wikipedia.org/wiki/Bill_ayers.

30 Sol Stern, "Obama's Real Bill Ayers Problem: The ex-Weatherman is now a radical educator with influence," in *City Journal*, April 23, 2008, http://www.city-journal.org/2008/eon0423ss.html.

31 Ibid.

32 Ibid.

33 Bill Ayers, Wikipedia, op. cit.

34 Bork, 262-263.

35 Mike S. Adams, *Welcome to the Ivory Tower of Babel: Confessions of a Conservative College Professor* (Augusta, GA: Harbor House, 2004).

36 Ben Shapiro, *Brainwashed: How Universities Indoctrinate America's Youth* (Nashville, TN: WND Books, 2004), 178.

37 Ibid., 179.

38 David Horowitz, *Indoctrination U: The Left's War Against Academic Freedom* (New York, NY: Encounter Books, 2004), 2.

39 David Horowitz, *Unholy Alliance: Radical Islam and the American Left* (Washington, D.C.: Regnery Publishing, Inc., 2004), 59. Horowitz provides additional insight on the nature of the contemporary Left movement in a post 9/11 world. He calls the Left "Neo-Communist," in its perspective. However, what distinguishes it from the former Communist movement is "its ad hoc attitude towards the revolutionary future, and the nihilistic agendas that follow. The contemporary Left defines itself and organizes its unity as a movement *against* rather than *for*. Its components may claim to be for egalitarian futures in which racism, sexism, and corporate dominance no longer exist and "social justice" prevails. But unlike Communists, contemporary leftists are not committed to even the rudimentary blueprint that they share in common as to what such an order might entail. It is this lack of programmatic consensus that leads some leftists to even deny that there is a "Left" and makes it possible for a fragmented coalition of Neo-Communists— including anarchists, eco-radicals, radical feminists, "queer" revolutionaries, Maoists, Stalinists, and vaguely defined "progressives"—to operate in improbable coalitions like the anti-war movement. It is why they can do so in ways that benefit such unlikely allies as Islamic radicals and the Ba'athist fascism of Saddam Hussein." (p. 59).

40 In 1915 the American Association of University Professors first approved a "Declaration of Principles on Academic Freedom and Academic Tenure, and then amplified it in 1940. In light of World War II, the AAUP declared that the use of classrooms for political agendas is a violation of academic freedom. Regulations against such activity are still published in faculty handbooks and even posted on official university websites. However, Horowitz has found that academic authorities are no longer enforcing these rules and students are mostly unaware of them (p. 4).

41 Horowitz, *Indoctrination*, 126.

42 Alliance Defense Fund, Center for Academic Freedom, http://www.centerforacademic freedom.org/about/default.aspx?cid=3.

43 Cornelius Van Til, "Creation: The Education of Man—A Divinely Ordained Need," in

Louis Berkoff and Cornelius Van Til, *Foundations of Christian Education: Addresses to Christian Teachers*, ed. Dennis E. Johnson (Phillipsburg, NJ: Presbyterian and Reformed Publishing Company, 1990), 44.

44   See endnote 12. Long gone are the days when the founders of America's colleges started with a vision such as the founders of Harvard College, who declared at its founding in 1643: "Let every Student be plainly instructed, and earnestly pressed, to consider well the maine end of his life and studies is to know God and Jesus Christ which is eternall life, Jn. 17:3, and therefore to lay Christ in the bottome, as the only foundation of all sound knowledge and Learning."

45   Cathy Lynn Grossman, "Young adults aren't sticking with church," *USA TODAY*, 8/07/2007, http://www.usatoday.com/printedition/life/20070807/d_churchdropout 07.art.htm.

Chapter Nine: Virtuous Citizens or Workers of the World?

1   John Dewey, "My Pedagogic Creed," in *American Progressivism: A Reader*, eds. Ronald J. Pestritto and William J. Atto, (Lanham, MD: Lexington Books, 2008), 131.

2   Allen Quist, *FedEd: The New Federal Curriculum and How It's Enforced* (St. Paul, MN: Maple River Education Coalition, 2002), 150.

3   Diane Ravitch, *National Standards in American Education: A Citizen's Guide* (Washington, D.C.: The Brookings Institution, 1995), 2.

4   Allen Quist, *America's Schools: The Battleground for Freedom* (Chaska, MN: EdWatch, 2005), 70.

5   Ibid., 57.

6   Ibid., 58-63, 69, 73.

7   Joel Spring, *American Education* (Boston, MA: McGraw Hill, 1998), 20-23.

8   Quist, *America's Schools*, 57-63.

9   Lynn M. Stuter, "The United Nations Connection to Washington State," May 1998, http://www.learn-usa.com/educationtransformation/stw005.htm.

10   Quist, *America's Schools*, 63.

11   Ravitch, 2.

12   Quist, *FedEd*.

13   Arne Duncan, "Secretary Arne Duncan Speaks at the 91st Annual Meeting of the American Council on Education," February 9, 2009, Department of Education, http://www.ed.gov/print/news/speeches/2009/02/02092009.html.

14   Ibid.

15   "Homeschooling Illegal" Declares German School Official, *Home School Legal Defense Association* website: http://www.hslda.org/hs/international/Germany/200501100.asp

16   Carolyn Moynihan, "British home-schoolers on notice to register," 15 Jun 2009, *Family Edge*, MercatorNet.com, http://www.mercatornet.com/family_edge/view/british_home_schoolers_on_notice_to_register/.

17   Spring, 20.

18   Eric Buehrer, *The Public Orphanage: How Public Schools Are Making Parents Irrelevant* (Dallas, TX: 1995), 60.

19   Quist, *FedEd*, 150.

20 Compulsory Education: Legislation and Laws, *National Conference of State Legislatures* website: http://www.ncsl.org/IssuesResearch/Education/CompulsoryEducation Overview/tabid/12943/Default.aspx

21 Martha M. McCarthy and Nelda H. Cambron-McCabe, *Public School Law: Teachers' and Students' Rights* (Boston, MA: Allyn and Bacon, Inc. 1987), 70.

22 Ibid.

23 Grace Chen, "The Public School vs. The Private School, *The Public School Review, http://www.publicschoolreview.com/articles/5.*

24 "Private Education in the United States," MSN Encarta, © 1993-2009 Microsoft Corporation. All Rights Reserved. http://encarta.msn.com/encyclopedia_1741500929/private_education_in_the_united_states.html.

25 Buehrer., 61.

26 "The Elementary and Secondary Education Act of 1965 forbids federally determined curricula." Hoover Institution - Daily Report Archives - Secretary Riley Reignites the Math Wars Retrieved from "http://en.wikipedia.org/wiki/Elementary_and_Secondary_Education_Act".

27 List of Goals 2000 educational goals:
    1. All children in America will start school ready to learn.
    2. The high school graduation rate will increase to at least 90 percent.
    3. All students will leave grades 4, 8, and 12 having demonstrated competency overchallenging subject matter including English, mathematics, science, foreign languages, civics and government, economics, the arts, history, and geography, and every school in America will ensure that all students learn to use their minds well, so they may be prepared for responsible citizenship, further learning, and productive employment in our nation's modern economy.
    4. United States students will be first in the world in mathematics and science achievement.
    5. Every adult American will be literate and will possess the knowledge and skills necessary to compete in a global economy and exercise the rights and responsibilities of citizenship.
    6. Every school in the United States will be free of drugs, violence, and the unauthorized presence of firearms and alcohol and will offer a disciplined environment conducive to learning.
    7. The nation's teaching force will have access to programs for the continued improvement of their professional skills and the opportunity to acquire the knowledge and skills needed to instruct and prepare all American students for the next century.
    8. Every school will promote partnerships that will increase parental involvement and participation in promoting the social, emotional, and academic growth of children. http://www.ncrel.org/sdrs/areas/issues/envrnmnt/stw/sw0goals.htm

28 Quist, *FedEd*, 16.

29 Ibid, 17.

30 Ibid.

31 A thorough critique of the 1995 edition is provided by Allen Quist in *America's Schools,*

93-100.

32   Center for Civic Education, Programs, *We The People: The Citizen and the Constitution*, Program Evaluation, http://www.civiced.org/index.php?page=program_evaluation.

33   Center for Civic Education, Publications, http://www.civiced.org/indexphp?page= national_standards_for_civics_and_government.

34   Quist, *America's Schools*, 20.

35   NCSS Curriculum Standards for Social Studies, National Council of the Social Studies, http://www.socialstudies.org/standards/taskforce/fall2008draft.

36   Ibid., 7.

37   Quist, *America's Schools*, 43.

38   Claudine Chalfant, "Global Warming Hype Sparks 'Eco-Anxiety' Syndrome," January 19, 2008, http://aftermathnews.wordpress.com/2008/01/19/global-warming-hype-sparks-eco-anxiety-syndrome/.

39   Marcelo M. Suárez-Orozco, "Globalization, Immigration, and Education," *Harvard Educational Review*, Vol. 71, No. 3, 347.

40   International Baccalaureate, The IB in partnership with governments and inter-governmental organizations, http://www.ibo.org/partnerships/governments/.

41   Global Research, "Bilderberg Plan For Remaking the Global Political Economy 2009" May 26, 2009, Market Oracle.co.uk, http://www.marketoracle.co.uk/index.php?name =News&file=article&sid=10903.

      George H. W. Bush, "Address Before a Joint Session of the Congress on the Persian Gulf Crisis and the Federal Budget Deficit," September 11, 1990, http://en.wikisource. org/wiki/Toward_a_New_World_Order.

      John Fonte, "Liberal Democracy vs. Transnational Progressivism: The Future of the Ideological Civil War Within the West," Appendix A in Allen Quist, *America's Schools: The Battleground for Freedom*, (Chaska, MN: EdWatch, 2005), 157-177.

42   W. Tullian Tchividjian, *The Kingdom of God: A Primer on the Christian Life*, (Glasgow, G.B.: Hay Nisbet Press, 2005) 41.

43   Rodney Stark, *The Victory of Reason: How Christianity Led to Freedom, Capitalism, and Western Success* (New York, NY: Random House, Inc., 2005), 234.

44   Philip Jenkins, *The Next Christendom: The Coming of Global Christianity* (Oxford: University Press, 2002).

45   Hillary Rodham Clinton, *It Takes a Village* (New York, NY: Simon & Schuster, 2006), xvi.

46   Barack Obama, "A World that Stands as One," in *Change We Can Believe In: Barack Obama's Plan to Renew America's Promise* (New York, NY: Three River Press, 2008).

47   Susan Hunt, *Heirs of the Covenant: Leaving a Legacy of Faith for the Next Generation* (Wheaton, IL: Crossway Books, 1998), 189.

48   Ibid.

Chapter Ten: Covenantal and Cultural Education

1   Susan Hunt, *Heirs of the Covenant: Leaving a Legacy of Faith for the Next Generation* (Wheaton, IL: Crossway Books, 1998), 48-49.

2   Robert D. Putnam, "Bowling Alone: America's Declining Social Capital," *Journal of*

Democracy, January 1995, 65-78.

3   Alan Wolfe, *One Nation After All* (New York, NY: Viking, 1998), p. 251.

4   "New Statistics on Church Attendance and Avoidance," March 3, 2008, Barna Group, http://www.barna.org/barna-update/article/18-congregations/45-new-statistics-on-church-attendance-and-avoidance.

5   Hunt, 48.

6   Henry R. Van Til, *The Calvinistic Concept of Culture* (Grand Rapids, MI: Baker Book House, 1972), 16.

7   Tullian Tchividjian, *Unfashionable: Making a Difference in the World by Being Different* (Colorado Spring, CO: Multnomah Books, 2009), 26.

8   Hunt, 47.

9   George Barna, *Transforming Children into Spiritual Champions: Why Children Should Be Your Church's #1 Priority* (Ventura, CA: Regal, 2003), 39. This should be the vision that guides our priorities of planning, stewardship, and ministry development at the local church level. But, as George Barna shows, only 24 percent of the senior pastors of the leading Protestant churches in the nation whom he interviewed set "ministry to children" as a top priority for the current year. Furthermore, Barna found that churches want a "turnkey curriculum" for their Sunday school classes. They want one that requires minimal preparation by the teacher and minimal prior knowledge by the students, but maximum provision of all the ideas, resources, and directions needed to fill the time children are in a class. Instead of being eager volunteers for these classes, parents would rather drop their kids off "so they can enjoy some time for their own spiritual nourishment and a break from their kids," says Barna. Consequently, he found that more than two-thirds of all Protestant churches he surveyed were struggling, according to their own admission, to recruit and retain adults to serve as instructors and helpers for their children's ministry.

10   Roy B. Zuck, *Precious in His Sight: Childhood and Children in the Bible* (Grand Rapids, MI: Baker Book House, 1996), 128.

11   Tchividjian, *Unfashionable,* 29.

12   Ibid., 26.

13   H. R. Van Til, *The Calvinistic Concept of Culture,* 29-30.

14   Ibid., 27.

15   Ibid., 19.

16   Ibid., 32.

17   D. James Kennedy and Jerry Newcombe, *Lord of All: Developing a Christian World-and-Life View* (Wheaton, IL: Crossway Books, 2005), 192.

18   George Barna, *Think Like Jesus: Make the Right Decision Every Time* (Nashville, TN: Integrity Publishers, 2003), 21.

19   George Barna, *Transforming Children into Spiritual Champions* (Ventura, CA: Regal, a division of Gospel Light, 2003), 34.

20   Ibid., 12.

21   Ibid., 18.

22   C. H. Spurgeon, *Spiritual Parenting* (Springdale, PA: Whitaker House, 1995), 7.

23   James W. Sire, *Habits of the Mind: Intellectual Life as a Christian Calling* (Downers Grove,

IL: Intervarsity Press, 2000), 206.

24   Cornelius Van Til, "Christianity and Culture: Christian View of Education (No Neutrality in Education)," Pt. 1, Mark 2:3-12, audio available at Westminster Theological Seminary, http://www.wts.edu.

25   "The Southern Baptist Convention Is Finally 'Throwing in the Towel' on Government Schools," Christian Newswire, June 2, 2009, http://www.christiannewswire.com/news/9859810513.html

26   Cornelius Plantinga, Jr., *Engaging God's World: A Reformed Vision of Faith, Learning, and Living* (Grand Rapids, MI: Wm. B. Eerdmans, Co. 2002), xi.

27   Karen L. Gushta, *Thomas Cranmer: Liturgical Reformer and Martyr for the Faith,* Unpublished paper. Knox Theological Seminary, Ft. Lauderdale, FL, Spring 2000.

28   Cornelius Van Til, *Essays on Christian Education* (Presbyterian and Reformed Publishing Co., 1974), 27.

Chapter Eleven: Conquering the Culture for Christ

1   Dennis Rainey, *A Call to Family Reformation* (Little Rock, AR: Family Life, 1996), 135.

2   Sam Kastensmidt, "Parents vs. the State," in *The Bible and the Blackboard: Biblical Solutions for Failing Schools,* by Gary Cass, Sam Kastensmidt, and Anthony Urti (Fort Lauderdale, FL: Coral Ridge Ministries Media, Inc., 2007), 71.

3   Adelle M. Banks, "Court: University of California can reject Christian school classes," *USA Today*, 8/15/08. http://www.usatoday.com/news/education/2008-08-15-christian-science_N.htm Larry Gordon, "A judge rules that the university system was not discriminatory in its refusal to count certain classes toward admission" *Los Angeles Times*, August 13, 2008. http://articles.latimes.com/2008/aug/13/local/me-uc13.

4   "Lawsuit Information: Update August 13, 2008," Calvary Chapel Christian School, Murrieta, CA, website, http://cccsmurrieta.com/secondary/lawsuit-info.asp.

5   United States Court of Appeals for the 9th Circuit, Wikipedia. http://en.wikipedia.org/wiki/United_States_Court_of_Appeals_for_the_Ninth_Circuit.

6   Christian schools are the majority of the nation's 27,000 private schools, which constitute 24 percent of all schools in the U.S.

7   Gary DeMar, *Whoever Controls the Schools Rules the World* (Powder Spring, GA: American Vision, 2007), 59.

8   George Barna, "Casual Christians and the Future of America," The Barna Group, Ltd., 2009, http://www.barna.org/barna-update/article/13-culture/268-casual-christians-and-the-future-of-america.

9   "AUSD School Board Approves LGBT Curriculum," *Action Alameda News*, May 27, 2009 http://actionalameda.org/actionalamedanewsblog/2009/05/27/ausd-school board-approves-lgbt-curriculum.

10   "Compulsory LGBT curriculum pushes 'political agenda' on school kids, California parents charge," *Catholic News Agency,* http://www.catholicnewsagency.com/new.php?=16090.

11   "School Board Forces LGBT curriculum on school children," *Temple Cleanser,* May 28,

2009, http://people.bakersfield.com/home/Blog/paxchristi3/45397.

12   Ibid.

13   Ibid.

14   Dennis Evanosky, "Board Votes to Instate New LBGT Curriculum," May 28, 2009, Alameda Sun, http://www.alamedasun.com/index.php?option=com_content&task=vie w&id=5238&Itemid=10.

15   *Catholic News Agency*, op.cit.

16   Kastensmidt, 72.

17   Arne Duncan, "Secretary Arne Duncan Speaks at the 91st Annual Meeting of the American Council on Education," February 9, 2009, Department of Education, http://www.ed.gov/ print/news/speeches/2009/02/02092009.html.

18   Lindsey Burke, "Does Universal Preschool Improve Learning? Lessons from Georgia and Oklahoma," *Backgrounder,* published by The Heritage Foundation, No. 2272, May 14, 2009. www.heritage.org/Research/Education/bg2272.cfm.

19   Burke, Heritage, op. cit.; Robert Holland and Don Soifer, "Federalizing Pre-K Could Do More Harm than Good," Issue Brief, April 29, 2009, *Lexington Institute,* http:// lexingtoninstitute.org/printer1406.shtml;
      "Universal Preschool Isn't the Silver Bullet: Reason TV video examines the arguments for and against universal pre-K," October 23, 2008, *Reason Foundation,* http://reason.org/ news/show/1003188.html;
      Amy K. Frantz, "For the Children? No, for the Politicians!" Policy Study No. 07-1, August 2007, *Public Interest Institute,* www.limitedgovernment.org.

20   Holland and Soifer, op. cit.

21   Obama Axes AmeriCorps' Inspector General, Was Criticized For Investigation Of Possible Misuse Of Funds By Sacramento Mayor, Obama Supporter, Washington, June 12, 2009,
      http://www.cbsnews.com/stories/2009/06/12/politics/main5082820.shtml?source=RSSa ttr=HOME_5082820.

22   Robert H. Knight, *Fighting for America's Soul* (Fort Lauderdale, FL: Coral Ridge Ministries Media, Inc., 2009), 54.

23   H.R. 1444, Congressional Commission on Civic Service Act, Sponsor, Rep. Jim McDermontt (WA-7th-D). Information on H.R. 1444 can be followed by searching for the bill at www.thomas.gov using the bill number.

24   Ibid.

25   "First Lady Michelle Obama, Cabinet Members Kick Off United We Serve," Press Release, June 22, 2009, United We Serve, www.serve.gov. http://www.nationalservice.gov/about/ newsroom/releases_detail.asp?tbl_pr_id=1382.

26   Examples of such discrimination are already taking place. See "E. Mich. Univ. ousts student for not affirming homosexual behavior" at the Alliance Defense Fund website. In this case the student was dismissed from his school's counseling programming for not affirming homosexual behavior as morally acceptable behavior. http://www. alliancedefensefund.org/news/pressrelease.aspx?cid=4899.

27   "Obama's Education Two Step," *In Our Opinion,* Center for Individual Freedom, CFIF. org, http://www.dfid.org/htdocs/freedomline/current/in_our_opinion/Obamas-

Education-Two-Step.html.

28   "Obama Administration Pushes CRC Ratification, June 24, 2009. *Parentalrights.org*. http://www.parentalrights.org/index.asp?Type=B_BASIC&SEC=%7B1F86E588-AA4A-43A1-998D-D9BF4FBE4D09%7D.

29   "'Child Rights' Forces Mobilize", Parentalrights.org, June 19, 2009, http://www.parentalrights.org/index.asp?Type=B_BASIC&SEC=%7B8281CDC6-F08F-4F69-B460-690BCE63FC7E%7D.

30   "Parental Rights Amendment Introduced in the United States Senate," Christian Newswire, June 22, 2009, 10:56 a.m. Sent from newsdesk@christiannewswire.ccsend.com. Christian Communications Network, 2020 Pennsylvania Avenue, NW, Washington, DC, 20006.

31   Ibid.

32   "20 Things You Need to Know About the UN Convention on the Rights of the Child," Parentalrights.org, http://www.parentalrights.org/index.asp?Type=BBASIC&SEC=%7BB56D7393-E583-4658-85E6-C1974B1A57F8%7D.

33   Michael Farris interview by John Rabe, Coral Ridge Ministries Media, Inc., June 2009.

34   Eric Buehrer, *Public Orphanage: How Public Schools Are Making Parents Irrelevant* (Dallas, TX: Word Publishing, 1995), 192.

35   Robert H. Knight, *Fighting for America's Soul* (Fort Lauderdale, FL: Coral Ridge Ministries Media, Inc., 2009), 123.

36   D. James Kennedy and Jerry Newcombe, *Lord of All: Developing a Christian World-and-Life View* (Wheaton, IL: Crossway Books, 2005), 131.

37   Cornelius Van Til, *Essays on Christian Education* (Presbyterian and Reformed Publishing Co., 1974), 7.

38   Ibid., 8.

39   Ibid.

40   D. James Kennedy, "The Incomparable Christ," in *Truths That Transform* (Fort Lauderdale, FL: Coral Ridge Ministries Media, Inc., 1996).

INDEX

212

214

ABOUT THE AUTHOR

KAREN L. GUSHTA is Research Coordinator for Coral Ridge Ministries of Fort Lauderdale, Florida. She has a long-standing love of education, both as a student and a teacher. She has taught at all levels, from kindergarten to graduate level teacher education.

After completing her first year of teaching on the Zuni Indian Pueblo in New Mexico, she obtained a masters degree in elementary education from the University of New Mexico. Subsequently she taught music and then 5th grade in North Carolina. She lived in Bogotá, Colombia for a year, where she taught English as a second language. In 1985, she started a graduate program at Indiana University with the goal of looking at foundational questions about teaching and learning. Earning her Ph.D. in Philosophy of Education with a minor in Instructional Psychology, Karen wrote her dissertation on "The Concept of 'Modeling' in Teacher Education."

After 15 years of teaching future and current teachers, Karen was led to leave higher education to work as the international director of the newly established ministry, Kids' Evangelism Explosion. In this role she carried on the work of developing curriculum and training seminars for children's ministry leaders around the world. When she left Kids' EE in 2004, it was established on every continent and translations of materials were underway in close to a dozen languages. Her experience the following year teaching kindergarten at Fort Lauderdale Christian School solidified her appreciation for the value of Christian education. Until then, although all of Karen's own undergraduate education had been at Christian schools, she had not taught in one.

Following her year as a kindergarten classroom teacher, Karen worked from home helping her husband Richard establish his business in the Fort Lauderdale area, where they now live. She also earned a masters degree in Christianity and Culture from Knox Theological Seminary in Fort Lauderdale, Florida. The program at Knox greatly extended Karen's biblical worldview perspective. Most notably, she gained a deeper understanding of the history of God's redemption of His people as revealed and recorded in Scripture. She also had the opportunity to read the great works of writers who have responded to God's written and His general revelation throughout history.

Much of Karen's enthusiasm for our call as Christians to transform culture can be attributed to her early Christian education and the multi-generational influences of her father, Nick R., and grandfather, Reinder Van Til. It was her grandfather who led her to Christ as a preteen with the simple question, "Do you love Jesus?" Although she lost sight of her confession for several decades, it was through the ministry of Coral Ridge Presbyterian Church and Dr. D. James Kennedy that Karen returned again to the foundation of her faith that had been established in her heart as a child and nurtured as a teen.

The War on Children is Karen's first book. She researched and wrote the booklet, *All the President's Men and Woman,* and edited several of the books in Coral Ridge Ministries' *Ten Truths* series. Karen also edited two books of sermons by Dr. D. James Kennedy, *The Mortgaging of America* and *Freedom From Financial Fear,* as well as the reprinted edition of *Truths That Transform,* all published by Coral Ridge Ministries. *Soli Deo Gloria.*